MAKING MEETINGS WORK

Many thanks
To Patrick for opening doors and inviting me in.
To Elizabeth who knows, without a doubt, that life is "wonderful, wonderful."
To my Mom for giving me the spirit to do this work.

ANN M. DELEHANT
with Valerie von Frank

MAKING MEETINGS WORK

How to Get Started, Get Going, and Get It Done

Foreword by Stephanie Hirsh

A JOINT PUBLICATION

nsdc

CORWIN PRESS
A SAGE Publications Company
Thousand Oaks, CA 91320

For information:

Corwin Press
A Sage Publications Company
2455 Teller Road
Thousand Oaks, California 91320
www.corwinpress.com

Sage Publications Ltd.
1 Oliver's Yard
55 City Road
London EC1Y 1SP
United Kingdom

Sage Publications India Pvt. Ltd.
B–42, Panchsheel Enclave
Post Box 4109
New Delhi 110 017 India

Printed in the United States of America

Library of Congress Cataloging-in-Publication Data

Delehant, Ann M.
Making meetings work: How to get started, get going, and get it done / Ann M. Delehant, with Valerie von Frank.
        p. cm.
Includes bibliographical references and index.
ISBN-13: 978-1-4129-1460-4 (cloth)
ISBN-13: 978-1-4129-1461-1 (pbk.)
    1. Business communication. 2. Meetings. I. von Frank, Valerie. II. Title.
HF57183.D43 2007
658.4′56—dc22

                                                        2006027351

This book is printed on acid-free paper.

06 07 08 09 10   10 9 8 7 6 5 4 3 2 1

Acquisitions Editor:	Rachel Livsey
Editorial Assistant:	Phyllis Cappello
Developmental Editor:	Valerie von Frank
Production Editor:	Melanie Birdsall
Typesetter:	C&M Digitals (P) Ltd.
Copy Editor:	Carla Freeman
Proofreader:	Ellen Brink
Indexer:	John Hulse
Cover Designer:	Rose Storey
Graphic Designer:	Scott Van Atta

Contents

List of Handouts

Foreword

Just imagine: You are invited to join the school improvement committee this year. You learn from colleagues of the significant contributions the committee makes toward the success of the school. You hear that members take their responsibilities seriously. New members receive orientation and mentoring to ease their transition on to the committee. Members arrive at meetings fully prepared and on time. A detailed agenda addresses meeting goals, topics requiring attention, an approach for addressing each issue, and desired outcomes. Discussions are characterized by mutual respect for contributions, thoughtful listening, problem solving, as well as an attitude of openness for possibilities as opposed to barriers. Decisions are captured and next-step actions and responsibilities are assigned. Assignments are completed in time for the next meeting. Participants look forward to meetings and the good things that occur because of their actions. Some even agree, on occasion, to additional meetings. As a result, you view it as an honor to accept the invitation to serve and are eager to get to work.

On the other hand, the following scenario could just as likely occur. Imagine being appointed as a new member of a committee. The member you replace hands you a disheveled notebook with papers from meetings held in the last five years. You try to review as much as possible in preparation for the first meeting. The first meeting starts 15 minutes late; the chair explains that the copy machine broke as he was trying to print the agenda. Everyone is introduced and encouraged to contribute to his or her degree of comfort. A colleague suggests that you spend most of the time at this first meeting observing rather than talking. Heeding this advice, you observe as a series of disjointed conversations occur. While the chair tries to manage the group, it is apparent that whoever speaks the loudest gains the attention of the group. On occasion, a motion is made and seconded, and a decision is reached. Everyone celebrates as items on the agenda are checked off and they near adjournment. The committee members appear more interested in finishing the agenda than in the potential impact of their efforts.

Unfortunately, it is more likely that educators have experienced the second scenario rather than the first. Educators have good intentions when they convene meetings. They see a need to share leadership, gather input, build ownership, accelerate action, and more. However, they generally make one of two mistakes. Either they assume good meetings just happen, or they fail to recognize the importance of good planning for meetings, to demonstrate respect for the time people contribute to the group. This book will help individuals who want to demonstrate that they value the time people give to meetings by applying effective meeting management skills. Educators will experience the first scenario I described above when leaders take advantage of the tremendous number of practical resources in this book.

Ann Delehant is a gifted meeting planner, consultant, facilitator, and coach. She has spent more than 25 years in education, helping educators reach their goals through meetings. She has experienced meetings through the lens of the participant, the convener, and the consultant. She has participated at local, state, and national levels and has served on appointed as well as elected committees. She knows firsthand what effective meetings can mean to a team, a school, or a school system, as well as the destructive potential of ineffective meetings.

In this book, Ann addresses five areas essential for ensuring successful meetings: planning a meeting, getting the group started, running the meeting, making decisions, and taking action. She has identified the critical issues effective leaders consider when convening people for the purpose of working together. For each issue, she offers an introduction and explanation. She brings the explanation to life through case studies and then provides ready-to-use tools and strategies to promote application.

The National Staff Development Council (NSDC) is the largest nonprofit membership association committed to ensuring success for all students through staff development and school improvement. Our goal calls for all teachers in all schools to experience high-quality professional learning and teamwork as part of each workday. NSDC leaders are confident that educators learn when they collaborate meaningfully and that as a result, students benefit. Effective meetings are key to effective collaboration. School leaders can ensure effective meetings, collaboration, and teamwork when they apply the skills and resources provided in this book. Purposefully planned meetings have the potential to produce focused dialogue and new understandings and behaviors that can positively impact team members and their students. *Making Meetings Work: How to Get Started, Get Going, and Get It Done* in the hands of meeting leaders will advance the goal of high-quality learning and performance by all students and educators.

—*Stephanie Hirsh*
Deputy Executive Director
National Staff Development Council

Preface

This book is designed for educators who find themselves needing to work in collaborative ways. For many who are used to working independently, this is a new way of doing business.

Today, when educators get together, they are less likely to be in a traditional meeting where information is dispensed to them and more likely to find themselves asking each other how they can better accomplish the challenges of improving student achievement.

For everyone who has ever asked, "Do we really need to have another meeting?" I have attempted to put together an outline that will help you answer that question. Sometimes the answer is no. In other cases, when meeting together can be beneficial, we need to develop the skills to make optimal use of our time.

In these pages, we look at how to decide whether getting a group together is the best way to accomplish the desired outcome, how to start a group, how to define the purpose of a meeting, and how to run an effective meeting. We review strategies for making decisions as a group and also review the steps for action plans.

Meetings can be valuable, helping develop a collaborative spirit; giving us an outlet for discussion, not just decision making; and changing the environment in which we work. It has been said that meetings are where an organization's culture perpetuates itself. If we adjust and improve what happens when we are together, we affect our own school culture and, ultimately, our ability to succeed with students in a high-pressured environment.

Groups are better than individuals alone for generating ideas and solving problems. Groups can help morale and help generate understanding, acceptance, and support for members. Acting as a group can help members sustain their support for the work and their own commitment. Group work can be a source of energy and renewal when the group is structured properly.

Just as there are different purposes for meetings, and some elements of this book will be appropriate to some of those and not to others, there also are different kinds of groups: elected groups, such as school boards, professional organizations, and boards of directors; appointed groups, such as advisory boards and committees; ad hoc or working groups, such as task forces or crisis intervention groups; and standing groups, such as school improvement committees, strategic-planning groups, grade-level teaching teams, and subject matter teams.

The issues and tools presented here can be used under different circumstances with many of the different groups. Facilitators working with any of the different groups should find some tools that will help in their work.

Planning, organizing, and carrying out our work in a collaborative setting (a meeting) is essential learning. Making efficient use of time spent working together is a necessity in our time-pressured society. We must learn how to use our time in groups and the skills to maximize what we can accomplish during that time.

This book is an attempt to assist in that effort.

Readers can browse through the highlighted tips for quick ideas to use in working groups; refer to the "Extended Readings" section to find texts that delve more deeply into specific needs, such as a book of "energizer activities"; and use the boxed pullouts for information that enhances specific topics within the text.

Each chapter contains steps outlining how to proceed with the issue at hand, from planning a meeting to creating an action plan. Follow the headlined steps to assist your own process, and use the handouts as tools when needed. The handouts included here offer forms and formats for tasks, such as voting, and for exercises, such as outlining the benefits and challenges of a planned option. These tools are reproducible for small groups.

While the topics are discrete, they are not entirely sequential. For example, one would certainly need to know about making decisions before convening a meeting. Readers may not be in groups that ever require action planning, or they may need to refer early to that chapter for a group set up specifically for that purpose. Each chapter builds on the last but can be read independently, as the reader needs.

Acknowledgments

I am expressive by nature. I build relationships easily and take delight in making new friends wherever I go. And so, finding ways to acknowledge all the people who have been my teachers, my colleagues, and my friends is impossible. Learning about facilitation, running effective and efficient meetings, and professional development has been a career-long journey for me. I have learned something in each and every school and with each and every group. In fact, I often say that one of my favorite things about my work is that I get to learn something new every day.

This path of mine began in the Rochester City School District when I was first hired as a performing arts teacher. The leaders of this project, Phale Hale, Larry Maynard, and Marlene Caroselli, invited me to participate in the leadership, grant writing, and design of this urban desegregation initiative. They opened a door, and I am forever grateful.

When people asked me in those early years what I wanted to be, I always had the same answer, "I want to be the Director of Staff Development." They always responded by saying, "We don't have a Director of Staff Development," and I always replied, "I know, but we will." Somehow I knew that "job title" would allow me to do work that matched my beliefs about developing capacity in our schools. Peter McWalters gave me the opportunity and the title, and what an amazing path that turned out to be for me. Gloria Frazier, from the International Center for Collaboration, taught me to facilitate by her example. Another amazing opportunity was provided by two loaned executives from Xerox Corporation, John Foley and Norm Deets, who introduced me to leadership through quality tools and also to Tom Kayser, author of *Mining Group Gold* and *Building Team Power*. He introduced me to formal meeting skills and facilitation tools. On another lucky day, representing the Rochester City School District at a meeting, I met Suzanne Meyer, who would become a fabulous friend and a creative ally.

I joined the National Staff Development Council (NSDC) that year, and at the first conference, Carlene Murphy met me at an elevator and invited me to my first annual meeting. "Wow" is the word that comes to mind about the 20 years of membership in this professional association. The NSDC vision of "every teacher, every school, every day" provides the challenge for all of us to stretch to meet this vision. It is through this organization that I have met some of my greatest teachers, many of whom have become great friends: Joellen Killion, Cindy Harrison, Jody Hoch, Rob and Kathy Bocchino, Joanne Quinn, Denny Berry, and the entire Fairfax team. The allies I have made, nationally and in the state of New York, support me and my work every day.

On another amazing day, I attended a conference on "New Roles for Central Office in a Decentralizing Environment," hosted by the National Education Association and the American Association of School Administrators. The facilitator of this program was Dr. W. Patrick Dolan, who invited me to join him as an associate of W. P. Dolan and Associates, a management/labor consulting group. He teaches me about systems and change, and about engagement and capacity building. He challenges me and encourages me, and I am forever indebted to him. He loves to tease me about the friends I have made as a result of our work together—and he is right. How else could I have met Pat Sweitzer, Kelli Wells, Ann Kilcher, Ed Quigley, and all the incredible educators we have worked with over the years?

My career has been filled with moments of invitation, opportunities to work with people who care deeply about the education of all children, and learning something new every day.

This book was first designed as the second edition of *Keys to Successful Meetings,* coauthored by Stephanie Hirsh, Sherry Sparks, and me. Their insights and ideas continue to guide my work today.

It is also important to recognize Joan Richardson, my NSDC editor, and, from Corwin Press, Rachel Livsey, my acquisitions editor; Carla Freeman, my copy editor; Melanie Birdsall, my production editor; and Valerie von Frank, my developmental editor. I needed more help than I could ever have imagined, and these incredible women walked me through the process. I am grateful for their patience and their insight.

When I reflect on this path of mine, I also want to recognize my family and dear friends and their contributions to the joy of my life. So, Ma, Buck and Karen, Marti, Amy and Peter, Jots, Elizabeth, Aimee and Matt, Julie and Eddie, Aunt Sally and Uncle Bud, Meg and Lauren, Debbie and Marty, Terry and Bob, and all in my circle, thanks for always loving me.

My current life takes me away from home more than some of them would prefer, and yet they support me each and every day. Some of us are just born lucky—I'm one of those lucky ones.

Corwin Press gratefully acknowledges the contributions of the following reviewers:

Lisa Fanning
Marriott Hospitality Center Coordinator
Montgomery College
Rockville, MD

Ronald L. Russell
Assessment Consultant/Licensed School Psychologist
Loess Hills Area Education Agency 13
Atlantic, IA

Susan N. Imamura
Principal
Manoa Elementary School
Honolulu, HI

Mary A. Connery
Director, Staff Development and Testing
Fairport Central School District
Fairport, NY

About the Author

 **Ann M. Delehant** is a caring educator and committed training and development professional. She is an experienced facilitator and staff developer, with deep school and district experience. Ann currently works as an independent consultant, serving as a facilitator, coach, trainer, and change agent. She addresses a variety of topics, including systems change, collaborative teamwork, coaching, facilitation skills, effective staff development practices, data/accountability, and long-range planning. She is frequently asked to serve as an external facilitator, assisting teams as they develop strategic work plans, solve problems, resolve conflicts, and make collaborative decisions. Ann recently completed training to develop skills as a life coach and is a founding member of Coaching School Results, Inc.

Ann is an associate of W. P. Dolan and Associates, a management and labor consulting firm that specializes in deep systemic change and collaborative work. In this role, she works with Dr. W. Patrick Dolan, supporting board of education, district, and union leaders who are committed to long-term reform initiatives. Ann has notable state and national affiliations. She is a senior consultant for and served as a Trustee of the National Staff Development Council (NSDC) and was a founding member of the New York State Staff Development Council. Ann received the NSDC Distinguished Service Award in 1996.

1

Planning a Meeting

A teacher friend of mine told me about a recent staff meeting she had attended. The faculty gathered in the school media center at the conclusion of a long and difficult workday. They grabbed bottles of water or a cup of coffee and sat down in hard plastic chairs around scattered tables. They exchanged pleasantries briefly, then faced the front as the principal spent three quarters of an hour giving updates, announcing decisions, and outlining his thinking about various issues facing the school and district. He paused for a restroom break, then provided a summary of the school's recent test results. My friend noticed several colleagues grading papers. Another, she said, was jerked awake by a peer. The teacher next to her completed a grocery-shopping list.

This meeting, while familiar to many, thankfully is no longer typical. More and more, group work is becoming a part of educators' work. We are leaving behind the isolationism that closed teachers off behind their individual classroom doors and forming groups with colleagues to collaboratively solve problems and focus collective time on student learning goals. As we do so, we must develop new skills to work together more efficiently and effectively. We need to spend more time working together, yet we feel pressed for time from all fronts.

Almost 70% of workers in organizations feel that meetings are unproductive, according to the 2005 Microsoft Office Personal Productivity Challenge, an online survey of more than 38,000 people worldwide. Respondents also said that ineffective meetings were one of the top impediments to productivity.

Contrast the meeting on the previous page with another I recently witnessed. In this one, also a meeting for teachers, the grade-level group met early in the day in the school library. The group gathered, facing each other around a large table. Substitute teachers covered the teachers' classes for the first half hour of the school day. As they arrived, teachers helped themselves to fruit and bagels and then quickly got down to work. A facilitator/recorder with chart paper was ready at the side. One member passed out samples of student work. The others knew from the group protocol how the meeting would proceed. After discussing the work for about 45 minutes and collaborating to improve the assignment, the teachers spent a few moments moving around in an energizing activity the facilitator had planned. They regrouped, summarized, and laid plans for their next meeting with a totally different focus and a more formal agenda.

Meetings can be productive when we follow some simple guidelines.

DECIDE WHETHER TO MEET

We *can* use meeting time to efficiently conduct work that advances learning goals. As a first step, we need to pause before scheduling another meeting to evaluate the benefits and weigh the real costs. Deciding whether a meeting is really necessary is the first step in beginning to "work smarter."

Tip: To begin to break the meeting habit, try hosting a 10-minute meeting or schedule a stand-up meeting. If standing becomes uncomfortable, the meeting is too long!

We first must ask whether there is a real reason to meet. Meetings too often are used simply to present information. In deciding whether to meet, ask, "Is there a different way to accomplish the same purpose?"

Using time wisely means forming groups only when the work warrants the involvement of those participating, when their knowledge and skills are needed to achieve the task. Before meeting, try asking, "What decisions need to be made by those who would be asked to spend time in this group?"

Ask, "Does the group have a clear purpose?"

If a meeting is not necessary, then try these strategies to accomplish the goal.

Share Information

• *"FYI" Copies of Minutes/Letters/Reports.* Rather than calling everyone to a meeting, include only key people and allow others to read the results. This is a useful strategy when a smaller group, such as a home-school relations committee, could accomplish the work and provide the results to the larger staff.

- *E-mail Messages.* E-mail is good one-way communication when a message needs to be sent immediately for receivers to be informed quickly. The tone of e-mails can be misconstrued, so pay attention to language and word choices. E-mail is a good tool for making announcements. Using e-mail depends on the culture of the targeted audience. You must be confident the group regularly uses this form of communication.

- *Voice Mail Messages.* Voice mail messages get the word out but can feel distant to the receiver. Use voice mail only when specific information needs to reach a number of people quickly or when the information is not important enough to warrant a conversation. This is a good means for conveying information but doesn't invite dialogue or build communication. A time to use voice mail might be when providing an update. Although voice mail has some associated negatives, it may still be more efficient than a full meeting.

- *Bulletin Board Messages in High-Traffic Areas.* Another form of one-way communication, posting flyers on bulletin boards, can convey key information in a time-efficient way. Posting information this way, however, does not ensure that the appropriate people have read it. The time to use such a posting is when information is less critical but still necessary, such as notice of an event.

- *Informal Newsletters.* Newsletters don't have to be designed or formatted. As a means to convey information, they may be nothing more than bulleted items in a list. This is another means of one-way communication when there is no need for dialogue or feedback and no action is expected from the recipients.

- *Weekly Bulletins.* Routine updates, such as often occur at staff meetings, can be easily dispensed in a written communication such as a weekly bulletin. Making this an ongoing communication alerts recipients that the information will be relevant and useful. This is a good venue for information about working conditions, rather than about the actual work of teaching and learning.

- *Intranets.* Many of the suggestions above, such as bulletins, newsletters, and messages, can be implemented online when schools are in the habit of using an internal Web site for communication or record keeping.

Collect Input or Stimulate Thinking

- *A Round-Robin Memo.* Send a memo with the information to a list of individuals. As each individual reads the memo, he or she can add notes to the bottom of the page. That person then checks off his or her name on the list of recipients and sends it along to the next person. Round-robin memos are useful for information that is necessary but not time-sensitive, such as letting others know about a proposed policy change and inviting feedback. Using a cover memo also helps ensure that targeted individuals have received the information.

• *Electronic Communications/Electronic Bulletin Boards.* This strategy is useful when dialogue is helpful and there is no pressing deadline for action. Bulletin boards might be used, for example, to receive feedback on an actual or proposed rule change.

Begin a Dialogue

• *Telephone Calls.* When the message needs to be personalized and a dialogue might ensue, the telephone is still a good choice. Although potentially more time consuming for the caller, it can ultimately save valuable resources by limiting others' time on the task. This is a good tool when there are a limited number of people involved, such as when a principal must make an immediate decision with input from key staff.

• *Informal Conversations ("Hall Talk").* The informal nature of conversation often helps build relationships while conveying information. If the information is not time-sensitive, hall talk can be a good alternative to a formal meeting. The downside of this informal form of communication is that it may not be systematic and so the information may not reach everyone, nor will people hear the information in any particular order. This can result in rumors. And for the people who were not included in the informal conversations, it can be seen as an exclusive process. Sensitive people will take it personally and may begin gossiping about who was included and who was excluded.

• *One-on-One Conversations.* If only a few key people actually are involved in the work and a decision must be made quickly or the issue is pressing, having individual conversations can be helpful to avoid a delay while trying to coordinate everyone's schedule. It is good for gathering input when one person is the decision maker. This tactic does not allow for group dialogue or brainstorming that might be helpful in problem solving.

After considering some of these options, you may find that you don't even need to schedule a meeting. If you have the authority and have decided a meeting or meetings are necessary, the following steps can help ensure that you achieve your desired outcome.

PLAN WITH A FEW COLLEAGUES

Sometimes, the work may benefit from the joint efforts and talents of your colleagues. With careful planning, you can achieve the goal and involve others. Begin by gathering a group of people who will help clarify and organize the tasks to be done.

This planning group should include just a few people who will help clarify the issues and identify needs. The planning group later may be merged with or supplanted by a larger working group that will carry out the group's purpose.

In an initial session, the planning group considers these guiding questions:

> **Tip:** Maximize efficiency by limiting the group size and involving only key stakeholders. Involve those who might feel excluded, delegate some of the work, and invite stakeholders' input in the process.

- What is the challenge or task we believe needs to be addressed?
- Is the need documented? What data support the issue?
- What is the desired outcome?
- Do the desired outcomes require the kinds of discussion and decision making that are best accomplished in a group?
- Are there other ways to achieve the desired outcome more efficiently?
- Who would participate in the group? Who would expect to or want to be present and represented?
- Who might feel entitled to participate?
- Will those affected by the project's outcome be willing to share ideas and information, and will they support the team's plans to meet the desired outcome?
- Who can best contribute to the desired outcome?
- When, where, and how often will the group meet?
- Is there enough time allocated to achieve the desired outcome?
- What are the costs (in staff time and resources) and the benefits of convening a group around this outcome?

You may want to select the appropriate questions for your team and post them on chart paper. Address the questions one by one, or have a more general dialogue and use the guiding questions to prompt discussion at key points. Be sure to cover the essential issues and decide whether forming a working group is the optimal way to address the identified need.

This initial discussion may last as little as 15 minutes or up to an hour, depending on the length and complexity of the issues. At the end of this session, be sure to thank members of this group for helping to clarify the task and ensure that the next steps are productive.

Determine the Group's Purpose

For every meeting, it is imperative to come up with a compelling statement that describes the purpose or at least one intended outcome. If nothing worthwhile seems to surface, the same will happen during the session.

Groups with a clear purpose are more likely to sustain member involvement and dedication to the task over time. Developing a purpose statement for the group's work is an essential component of creating commitment. If members do not feel an emotional, moral, or ethical response to the group's purpose, they are less likely to be deeply involved enough in the work to help produce a quality result. As Michael Fullan (2001) states, "Focusing on outcomes clarifies for teachers and principals what they are trying to accomplish and drives backward through the process toward moral purpose" (pp. 117–118). A strong commitment between and among group members to produce high-quality results is key to getting the job done well. That cohesiveness comes about through having a clear purpose.

Katzenback and Smith (1986) state that the best teams invest time and effort into exploring and shaping a specific purpose that everyone in the group can agree with and translate into the group's performance goal. Sometimes, determining the group's purpose is a simple process; there is a clear outcome, a clear need. At other times, the process of developing a purpose is more complex and involves more group discussion of the issue.

If the group needs more discussion, consider these questions:

- What work is the group expected to do?
- What key decisions have to be made to accomplish that work?
- Is there an expected product?
- Who is the recipient of the product?
- How will the product be used?
- Who will be affected by the outcome of the work?
- What is the relationship and alignment of the purpose to the organization's goals?
- Where does the group fit in the hierarchy of the organization?
- Are there any preconceived opinions of the group's task by group members or others?
- Who has veto power over the group's recommendations or decisions?
- How much time will the group need to complete the task?
- What are the implications if the group does not accomplish its task?
- What resources are available to help the group accomplish its goal?
- When will the group disband? Is it a standing committee or a task force?

The answers to these questions not only help clarify the group's purpose but also contain essential information to provide to potential members when inviting them to be part of the work.

Consider the Nonpurpose

While teams are defining a purpose, some also find it useful to define the *nonpurpose*. A nonpurpose states what is off-limits. Knowing what the group is *not* going to address can greatly increase the group's effectiveness. Groups often state a purpose but rarely clarify the nonpurpose.

A nonpurpose clearly identifies issues that the group might be tempted to discuss but that will not further the process or help the group achieve its goals. For example, if the group's purpose is to "Create a new schedule for the middle/high school within the budget constraints," the nonpurpose might be, "We will not discuss the contractual issues that need to be resolved before implementing the new schedule." Or when a group is meeting to "Discuss the role of literacy coaches and their work in classrooms," members may state their nonpurpose as, "We will not discuss the effect of the principal's resignation on the work of the coaches." While leadership changes may be related to the role of the coach, the team has no authority to select the new principal. Stating the nonpurpose keeps the group from spending time on an issue it cannot control.

If nonpurposes don't arise naturally, don't force them. You can add to them during sessions when they pop up in discussion. Don't be surprised if you have more nonpurposes than purposes during a particular session. Remember, "non" is not negative. Putting some issues outside the group's concern ensures that its focus is clear. The greater the clarity, the greater the results. Nonpurpose statements keep groups from spinning their wheels or getting off track.

As group members are defining the purpose and nonpurpose, continue to ask them to comment, ask questions, identify concerns, and reach group understandings.

Decide Who Writes the Purpose Statement

Discuss with planning-group members whether the planning group or working group needs to write the purpose statement.

Having the planning group define the purpose and present it later to the working group as a finished product gives the working group a clear starting point and allows it to immediately focus on the work. Having a purpose statement in hand also means one less meeting for the larger working group, a more efficient use of more people's time. However, without being involved in writing the purpose, some group members

> **Tip:** If the planning group writes the purpose statement, be sure to revisit the purpose with the working group at the first meeting.

may not feel the level of commitment to the product they would have had they been involved in creating the purpose statement.

Write a Formal Purpose Statement

If the goal or need is not particularly complex, the purpose statement may have become clear as the planning group answered the guiding questions for deciding whether it was necessary to meet. For more complex issues, the group may need more discussion for members to clearly state the group's purpose.

When the group is ready to prepare a formal purpose statement or mission, provide several samples before beginning to take ideas. (See Handout 1.1: Sample Purpose Statements.)

Purpose statements should be short, clear, and specific. The following are some examples:

- The sixth-grade team will develop 10 common assessments for mathematics. They will use the data from the assessments to guide instructional planning.
- This group will examine the K–12 writing program, evaluate resources, and make recommendations to the English language arts director and assistant superintendent for curriculum and instruction for improvements to the K–12 writing program.
- The committee will analyze student data and staff needs and develop the professional development priorities for the school year.

Tip: As the group prepares its purpose statement, be sure members understand whether the group is advisory or has authority as a decision-making body.

Continue the Discussion

- *Ask for Questions.* Once the group has written its purpose statement, ask participants to contribute any remaining questions by writing them on index cards. Take time to respond to questions, and research any unanswered questions to present at a future meeting.

- *Continually Assess Commitment.* When a group meets over a long period of time, members may find it necessary to revisit the purpose and the outcomes the group desires to ensure that members maintain their clarity and commitment still exists. Assessing the group's commitment to the purpose can be a useful periodic checkup. A quick check of group members' reactions to a few simple questions using the Likert scale can help keep the group on track. (See Handout 1.2: Analyzing Group Commitment.)

- *Keep the Purpose Out Front.* Revisit the group's purpose statement at the beginning of each successive meeting. Write the group's purpose statement at the top of the agenda or on chart paper to post at each meeting. Some groups also have their members sign the chart as a team-building exercise. The symbolism of adding signatures to the purpose statement is sometimes helpful to building group commitment.

SELECT GROUP MEMBERS

Having the right people represented in the group is crucial to its success. Katzenbach and Smith (1986) define a *team* as a small number of people with complementary skills who are committed to a common purpose, performance goals, and common approach for which they hold themselves mutually accountable.

HANDOUT 1.1: SAMPLE PURPOSE STATEMENTS

This group will assess the current quality of K–12 student writing in the _____ school district and make recommendations to _____ for program improvements.

This group will generate a list of methods of assessing student learning outcomes and provide models/samples of each form of assessment.

The sixth-grade team will develop 10 common assessments for mathematics and use the data from the assessments during grade-level team meetings.

This group will study current available data for meeting the needs of gifted and talented students in regular classrooms. The group will examine research-based strategies and develop a plan to meet the needs of students in Grades 3 through 8.

Sample Purpose and Nonpurpose Statements

Group: Data liaisons will examine school and district and student/staff data and will make recommendations for staff development priorities.

Purpose: This group will make recommendations to the superintendent's cabinet regarding ways to improve the recruitment, selection, and induction procedures for new employees.

Nonpurpose: This group will not discuss the costs necessary to recruit needed staff.

Group: The Learning Team will examine school and district and student/staff data and will make recommendations for staff development priorities.

Purpose: The Learning Team will prepare a long-range district plan for staff development.

Nonpurpose: The Learning Team will not challenge the state requirements for licensure.

Group: The district leadership team is working to pass a bond levy.

Purpose: To get one more vote than the opposition.

Nonpurpose: To energize the opposition.

HANDOUT 1.2: ANALYZING GROUP COMMITMENT

Directions

Using a four-point Likert Scale, ask participants to assess their commitment to the purpose of the team. The information can then be examined in light of how all members view the group's purpose/goals and how they have been formulated.

Statement	Strongly Agree	Agree	Disagree	Strongly Disagree
1. I support the purpose of this team.				
2. The purpose of this team is clear.				
3. I had an opportunity to formulate or influence the purpose of this team.				
4. The team periodically reviews and revises its goal.				
5. The purpose of this team meets my individual needs.				
6. The purpose of this team meets an organizational need.				
7. The team has the capacity to accomplish this goal.				
8. I can clearly state the purpose of this team.				

SOURCE: From *Building Systems for Professional Growth: An Action Guide*, by Margaret A. Arbuckle and Lynn B. Murray, Regional Laboratory for Educational Improvement of the Northeast & Islands, 1989. Copyright by WestEd. Reprinted with permission of WestEd, www.wested.org.

Give careful thought to who needs to be invited to the group. Effective work depends on members' blend of skills and knowledge, their backgrounds and personalities, and the level of commitment they bring to the project. The group must also be structured to represent the necessary stakeholders.

Decide on Group Characteristics

The planning group begins to form the working group by discussing and deciding on key characteristics:

• *Size.* Different-sized groups have advantages and disadvantages, some of which are represented in Table 1.1. The most important determinant of group size is that the number allows for representation of appropriate roles, responsibilities, and perspectives. Provide a range for the ideal number in the group to allow some flexibility as the group is assembled.

Table 1.1   Advantages and Disadvantages of Group Sizes

Group Size	Advantages	Disadvantages
2–7	• Easy to assemble quickly • Informality is possible • Flexible and creative • Group dynamics are manageable	• May have limited viewpoint • Numbers may not exist for the group to have more creative ideas
8–15	• Most conducive to synergy • Everyone can participate • Can be informal and spontaneous	• Complexity of group dynamics increases • Consensus may take longer • Needs facilitator and recorder
16–30	• Ideal for information sharing • Provides opportunities for information sharing • Increases potential for ownership and commitment • Provides larger number of potential leaders for various projects • Ensures anyone who wishes to serve has the opportunity	• Requires a facilitator • Needs ground rules • Needs small work groups to keep everyone involved • Needs to change small work groups often to prevent powerful cliques from forming

• *Diversity.* Representation is critical in forming the group. Include representatives from all areas of the organization that could be affected by the group's decisions. Consider the following:
  – Gender
  – Years of experience
  – Types of experience
  – Race
  – Ethnicity

Also consider people who have different roles, titles, and experiences and who work in different parts of the system and at different levels of authority. W. Patrick Dolan (1994) refers to this as "constituency engagement" or "diagonal" team planning. Consider the following criteria:

– Organizational level (site based, departments, central office)
– School level (preschool, elementary, middle, high school, adult education)
– Assignment (administrative, teaching, support staff, paraprofessional, etc., as well as teaching assignment, such as core teachers, special education, special subjects)
– Geographic/regional representation
– Community representation

• *Skills and Expertise.* The collective expertise within the group will determine its ultimate success. Determine the kinds of expertise the group needs. For example, if the group is responsible for developing a comprehensive math/science grant application, participants might include representatives from curriculum development, professional development, school-based leaders, math and science teachers, program evaluators, and the finance department.

Discuss who can provide the process as well as the content skills necessary to accomplish the goals. The group might need a skilled facilitator, for example, if no one on the planning team fills that role. Someone with particular knowledge of research relevant to the group's purpose or expertise in collaboration might be what the team needs.

Clarify the Selection Process

Determine who needs to be at the table and how you will find those individuals. Participants may be targeted as follows:

• *Invited.* The advantage of inviting group members is that the planning group or group chairperson controls the membership. A disadvantage is that some of those who might be interested in the group's work could be excluded. Others might be disappointed not to be asked to participate.

• *Appointed.* School or system leaders may want to be involved in the group's work by appointing members. The advantage of appointing members is that since the invitation comes from higher-ups, invitees might feel a certain prestige at being asked to serve. Disadvantages are the same exclusions that occur with invited participation.

Another way to appoint members is identify groups that need to be represented and invite the leaders to appoint participants to represent their groups. For example, say the planning group decides it wants representative teachers and parents. The group asks the professional association/union president to identify teachers from the association, department, or grade-level chairpersons to identify department representatives and asks the Parent Teacher Association president to select parent representatives.

- *Volunteers.* Soliciting volunteers who meet the preestablished criteria for membership is another option. A disadvantage of this process is the disappointment caused when individuals who volunteer are not selected to serve. However, the commitment of those who do serve is greater since they ask to be part of the group.

A different option in selecting volunteers is to explain the membership requirements, such as having a certain stated expertise, attending regular meetings, completing prework assignments, and committing to a consensus process, then allowing all to serve who agree to meet the requirements. The chairperson must be prepared to use a facilitator if the group's size becomes too large.

Another idea is to announce a meeting and allow anyone attending to become part of the group. If the group needs greater diversity, members can solicit others to join.

Solicit Nominations

Whether members are invited or volunteer, it is useful for the group to have strategies for determining who should be part of the work. Several steps can aid in this process. The planning team may wish to create a nomination form for potential volunteers or invitees to submit. The form can provide the group with the information necessary to help select the final group members.

Make sure that the nomination form includes questions about the key areas the planning group discussed as necessary criteria for involvement, such as the individual's background, role, expertise, and skills.

Rate Your Candidates

Develop a matrix to help visualize who is at the table and potential members' balance of strengths. Create similar matrices whenever a new group is being formed and specific criteria need to be addressed. (See Handout 1.3: Sample Matrix of Selection Criteria.)

After filling in and reviewing the matrix, the planning group might find that specific needs have not been met for the group. Planners may want to develop an individual job description for that need. For example, a school leadership team might announce,

> We are seeking a community member to serve on the school leadership team. The representative will be someone who is a recognized community leader, an effective facilitator, an advocate for positive change, and willing to serve as the "healthy skeptic." A background in research and evaluation would be helpful.

The planning group then can let others know the group's specific needs. Be careful to maintain confidentiality for all documents.

HANDOUT 1.3: SAMPLE MATRIX OF SELECTION CRITERIA

Each team can prepare a matrix detailing criteria to ensure that the right people serve on the team. You can create a "job description" to assess potential candidates against the criteria. When the planning team meets, they can identify the needs of the project and clarify the expectations of the group participants.

In this example, a school leadership team is being formed. It might be helpful to include a person who has the following characteristics:

- Is willing to take on additional leadership responsibilities
- Is able to analyze and interpret data
- Is willing to commit to additional professional development
- Is a recognized school/community leader
- Is an effective facilitator
- Is able to engage others to achieve the school goals
- Values processes for planning, implementing, monitoring, and evaluating results
- Is an advocate for positive change
- Has expertise in writing grants
- Serves as the "healthy skeptic"
- Is a team player

Criteria	Dwayne	Ellen	Sharon	Jay	Denny
Is willing to take on additional leadership responsibilities					
Is able to analyze and interpret data					
Is willing to commit to additional professional development					
Is a recognized school/community leader					
Is an effective facilitator					
Is able to engage others to achieve the school goals					
Values processes for planning, implementing, monitoring, and evaluating results					
Is an advocate for positive change					
Has expertise in writing grants					
Serves as the "healthy skeptic"					
Is a team player					

Finalize the Membership

If the planning group is selecting members, finish the work by having members consider some key questions:

- Do team members have the expertise and authority needed to carry out the task?
- Are all individuals who have a stake in the team's decisions included?
- Do team members' personalities and styles balance?
- Would these individuals have a personal interest or stake in the team's work?
- Which levels of the organization are represented, and how will the different roles affect the team?

If members are being appointed, send official notification of the appointment from a leader in the organization (see Figure 1.1).

When group members are being invited or volunteers are selected, ask the chairperson of the planning group to write or speak with the potential members. Let them know the benefits of being part of the work. As part of the group, they will have the following opportunities:

- To influence the direction of the organization
- To work with esteemed colleagues
- To actively participate in professional development associated with group work

Figure 1.1   Sample Letter of Appointment

Dear Sam,

Congratulations on your appointment to serve on the curriculum-mapping team for K–12 mathematics. Your leadership and commitment to staff development as a math coach contributed to your appointment and recognition by the Division of Curriculum and Staff Development for this honor.

We look forward to working with you over the next 18 months on this important task. We trust you will find the work a learning experience and pleasurable responsibility. You will be working closely with our associate superintendent for curriculum, a state advisor, and other K–12 district math experts. They will provide the support necessary to make this a model process.

Thank you again for accepting this appointment. Math teachers throughout the district will benefit from the leadership you offer the organization.

Sincerely,

Joseph F. Frazier

Cc (Superintendent's name)

Finally, ask the chairperson of the planning group to send members a separate letter identifying financial agreements, acknowledging how they will be reimbursed for expenses associated with the group work and whether they will be paid for their time. Be sure to discuss any financial aspects of their involvement at the initial group meeting.

Plan for Ways to Replace Members

When a member leaves the group, choose new members based on the skills and expertise needed by the group. If the group's responsibilities change or grow, the group may have to add new members who have skills and expertise in areas that meet the new needs.

Determine Whether the Group Will Have a Chairperson

Discuss whether the group needs a chairperson. Some chairs are appointed by the group or the individual responsible for forming the group. Some become chairpersons because of their positions outside the group, such as school leader. Determine how the group will select a chairperson if necessary.

BUILD THE AGENDA

According to a MCI Conferencing (1998) white paper, three out of four respondents consider having a prepared agenda extremely important to any meeting. The study also found a direct correlation between preparation, particularly of the agenda, and meeting productivity.

Developing an effective agenda is a skill. A well-planned agenda lets participants know the goals of the meeting and the steps the group will take to achieve it. It is a roadmap for the time the group will spend, a reminder afterward of what occurred, and a planning tool for follow-up action.

An online survey found that the main reasons employees dread meetings is that the work doesn't lead to decision; participants aren't prepared; the meeting doesn't start or end on time; and the agenda isn't followed (Bertagnoli, 1999).

Tip: Vary the meeting time for a standing group to maintain interest. Survey the group to determine their preferred times, dates, locations, and methods for communication (e-mail, mail, phone call, etc.).

A well-prepared agenda clearly states the meeting's objective, issues to be discussed, beginning and ending times, location, participants, and what is expected of each in preparing for the meeting. The agenda is the tool for creating a meeting that works. It is designed to ensure that the group is both effective and efficient.

Include Key Elements

The best agendas include several main components:

- *Topic.* A brief description of the issue or item to be discussed.
- *Responsible Person.* The person who will lead the discussion of the topic. This does not imply the person who will manage the initiative; it does acknowledge who will facilitate the process during the meeting.
- *Desired Outcome.* The goal or purpose so that the facilitator and team members clearly understand what must be accomplished. This is the most important element of the agenda. The desired outcome is written as a neutral statement, not one that seems to predict or predetermine the outcome of the discussion. For example, the desired outcome statement would not be "Approve offering university credit for conference attendance." Instead, it would be phrased "Determine whether to offer university credit for conference attendance."
- *Timeline.* The amount of time allotted to the issue. To keep the group on task, reference the actual hour and minutes rather than a generic number of minutes. For example, write "9:45 a.m. to 10 a.m." rather than "15 minutes." The clock will keep you on target, whereas the number of minutes can lead to sloppy time-keeping.
- *Members' Involvement.* Notations identifying the expected involvement from group members. For example, (I) might indicate an information item, (D) a discussion/dialogue item, (A) an action item, or (DP) a decision point. Items might be grouped together under a heading on the agenda.

These key elements are universal, no matter what format the agenda takes.

Review Alternate Formats

Three modified agenda formats are available in handouts. (See Handout 1.4: Purpose/Nonpurpose Agenda Format; Handout 1.5: Contemporary Agenda Format; and Handout 1.6: Boxed-Agenda Format.)

- *The purpose/nonpurpose agenda* planning format helps the team stay focused by specifying issues that will and will not be discussed.
- *The contemporary agenda* format is most useful for an established group with clearly understood rules and ground rules.
- *The boxed-agenda* format is a more traditional form. By listing desired outcomes, it can help groups in the earlier stages of development follow the format.

(Text continues on page 21)

HANDOUT 1.4: PURPOSE/ NONPURPOSE AGENDA FORMAT

Although the team will have clarified the purpose and nonpurpose during the process of establishing the team, it is always good to review these items with the team during the initial meeting(s). Ensure that there is agreement on the purpose and nonpurpose.

At this time, discuss the types of agenda items that will be included and those that will be avoided or forwarded to another work group.

Team:

Members:

Date:

Purpose of the group:

Types of agenda items that will be considered:

Nonpurpose of the group:

Types of agenda items that will not be considered:

HANDOUT 1.5: CONTEMPORARY
AGENDA FORMAT

Group:

Participants:

Date: _____ Time: _____ Location: _____

Item	Type	Person Responsible	Time	Desired Outcome
Welcome, Continental Breakfast			8:00	
LEARNING: Application	D	Sue	8:30	Discuss how to use ideas from *Making Meetings Work* as part of our team work.
Purpose	A	MaryJo	9:30	Review the purpose/nonpurpose statements. Make a commitment to the priorities.
Retreat	A	Dudley	10:00	Choose the location for the summer retreat. Identify and agree to the themes for the retreat. Seek volunteers to serve on the planning team to design the summer retreat.
Break			10:45	
Committee Reports	D/A	Kelli Patrick Ann	11:00	Present the latest news from each of the standing committees. Determine next steps.
Strategic Plan Report Action Team Reports Annual Update Evaluation of Plan	D	Amy	1:00	Share action plan reports. Introduce the format for the annual update. Determine how to evaluate the plan.
Debrief	D	Josh	2:45	Discuss progress made during the day. Critique attention to the purpose and the norms. Complete plus/delta.
Next Steps Wrap-up	A	Vanessa	3:00	Define next steps. Identify topics for next meeting.

Attachments:
Committee Reports:
Articles:
Schedule:

HANDOUT 1.6: BOXED-AGENDA FORMAT

Agenda:

Team:

Participants:

Date/Time: _____   Location: _____

Chairperson: _____   Facilitator: _____

Recorder: _____   Time Keeper: _____

Next Agenda Builder: _____

Purpose of Team:

Topic	I/D/A*	Desired Outcome	Facilitator	Start Time[+]

*I: Information, D: Discussion, A: Action/Decision Point

[+]Clock Time

Bring Your Calendar

Discuss with the planning group the pros and cons of each sample format. Use the ideas from these samples to modify the format to meet the group's needs, but retain the key elements.

Decide Who Sets the Agenda

Initially, a planning group or facilitator may decide the agenda for a meeting. If the group is an ongoing group, provide an opportunity for members to discuss how future agendas will be set.

The agenda can be determined by the group leader or facilitator, or it can be developed by a representative committee or individual.

Some groups leave developing the agenda to the group leader. If the leader has the task of preparing the agenda, some participants will feel that the old model of top-down authority is in place. Leaving the task to an effective leader, however, can streamline the process and allow the leader or facilitator to help effectively move the group toward the desired outcome.

Other groups have a subgroup set the agenda. New teams or low-trust teams (teams that for some reason have little trust in the process; for example, their confidence in their leader has somehow been compromised) often put the job of agenda planning into the hands of a representative group. A subcommittee is especially useful when conflicting priorities exist and decisions have to be made regarding the agenda because of limited time. Using a subcommittee to set the agenda takes additional time and coordination.

Some groups decide to delegate authority for the agenda to an individual member. High-trust teams (teams that have built trust in one another and in the process) most often give the job of the agenda builder to one team member. The responsible individual holds a great deal of authority within the group in this way, and this person may face some challenges if conflicts arise over what has been or will be put on the agenda.

Finally, the group as a whole can be involved in setting the agenda. Using everyone's time and attention in this way, however, may not be the most efficient or effective method.

It is important that teams make conscious decisions about how the agenda will be set so that all team members feel they have input and confidence in the process.

Develop the Content

The content of the agenda can be decided as follows:

- Based on the stated purpose and the identified needs of the group
- Based on participants' input ahead of the meeting
- Decided by group members at the beginning of the meeting or at the end of the previous meeting
- Based on minutes from prior meetings
- Some combination of these styles

Gather Suggestions

If the group decides to gather input, develop a process to facilitate collecting members' suggestions. Be sure the group is committed to using members' ideas if input is allowed.

Develop a format for participants to submit agenda items. As you develop the format, include areas for responses to these guiding questions:

- What is the topic to be discussed?
- Is the item an information item, a discussion item, or one that needs a decision or action from the group?
- How much time is needed?
- Who is responsible for presenting the issue? Who will lead the discussion?
- What is the desired outcome of the dialogue?
- Are there others who are not members of the group who would be helpful to the discussion and could be invited to be present or participate in the problem solving or decision making?
- What is the rationale for including this topic on the agenda? Is it aligned with the team's purpose?

As a group, decide who is able to submit items for consideration—members only, or others not on the team, such as other faculty, students, parents, and administrators. Set clear deadlines for requests to put items on the agenda. (See sample forms for gathering input: Handout 1.7: Agenda Input Format 1 and Handout 1.8: Agenda Input Format 2.)

Tip: Send the agenda to meeting participants at least 48 hours prior to the meeting to ensure that everyone is prepared.

After reviewing the elements of the different forms, have the planning group discuss their pros and cons and design a format that meets the needs of the members.

Once the group has decided to accept suggestions, it is important for the individual or group deciding whether to include these items on the agenda to follow through. If a topic will not be included on the agenda, provide immediate feedback to the person suggesting the item about what is happening to the item. For example, the topic was forwarded to a subcommittee for further study, forwarded to an individual staff member for his or her action, is being returned for clarification, or did not match the group's identified priorities and therefore cannot be addressed at this time.

Various forms of technology can support the group in gathering agenda input. For example, e-mail could be used to request suggestions from group members. More sophisticated methods of gathering input include electronic polling tools, a discussion board, or an interactive form. Any of these would only be appropriate within an environment where team members habitually use that technology.

HANDOUT 1.7: AGENDA INPUT FORMAT 1

Topics or ideas for the _____ meeting

Please send or fax to:

Phone:

Fax:

Name of Person Submitting Topic: _____

Check One:

Information _____ Discussion _____ Decision/Action _____

Desired Outcome (a statement of what you hope to accomplish at the meeting)

_____

_____

_____

Others who should be included in the meeting: _____

_____

Action Taken:

_____ The topic will be included on the agenda at the meeting on _____. You have _____ minutes on the agenda. Please be prepared with materials for _____ people. Please submit any prework or information for team members to _____ before _____. This will ensure that team members are prepared for the discussion.

_____ The topic was forwarded to _____.

_____ The topic, while important, does not meet the stated purpose of this team, so it cannot be considered at this time.

_____ Other: _____

HANDOUT 1.8: AGENDA INPUT FORMAT 2

Use this format to suggest items for upcoming meetings.

Idea Submitted By:

Name: _____   Role: _____

Phone: _____   Fax: _____

Topic	I/D/A*	Desired Outcome	Preferred Date	Time Needed

*I: Information, D: Discussion, A: Action/Decision Point

Others who should be present for the discussion: _____

_____

Use this space to inform the person who submitted the topic for consideration of the outcome. Let him or her know whether the issue will be addressed on an upcoming agenda, was sent to subcommittee, or was addressed in another way.

TO: _____   FROM: _____

Topic	Disposition

Impromptu Agendas

For informal meetings or for those called in the midst of change, building the agenda at the start of the meeting is an effective strategy. The group leader can poll group members at the meeting's start for items they want to cover. Build the agenda from this list, prioritize the issues, and set a limit for the meeting time.

Using a "Parking Lot"

During the meeting, issues may arise that are important but are not part of the current agenda. The facilitator may keep a running list of issues and ideas that are generated on a "parking lot" chart. Facilitators may also keep index cards on the table for participants to record their ideas during the meeting. The parking lot is a public acknowledgment of issues that are not part of the current discussion. Some people prefer to see their ideas recorded on charts as a reminder for later discussion. Others may be happy to have a process for identifying important ideas.

The list of items that have been raised during the meeting may need to be addressed at another meeting. Distribute this list from the parking lot chart or the index cards with the minutes. Those responsible for setting the agenda may find important ideas on this list to place on the next meeting's agenda.

A Standing Format

Some standing groups might use an agenda that follows the same format, for example, approval of the minutes, followed by old business, new business, and evaluation. Other groups have reports from standing committees. Remember to share written reports, minutes, or highlights so that group time is not spent just sharing the data. Instead, invite the standing committees to present issues for decision making or to gather information. Individual group members then can add specific items, either by submitting them to the group in advance in writing or at the beginning of the meeting.

Create the Agenda

A great agenda is closely tied to the meeting's objective, and participants feel its relevance to the work. Whoever is setting the agenda must anticipate and plan for relevance. Ask three questions:

- To achieve our objective, what do we need to do in the meeting?
- What conversations will be important to the people who attend?
- What information will we need to begin?

Here is a list of ideas for the chairperson or subgroup setting the agenda to consider:

- *Review all suggestions for agenda items.* Decide which to include by asking which will advance the achievement of the team's purpose.

- *Determine which items could be dealt with in another way.* Remember that meetings are often not the best way to share information. You may save a considerable amount of time if you establish consistent alternative processes for information sharing. Save meeting time for dialogue, data analysis, problem solving, and decision making.

- *Analyze items.* Are the items ready to bring to the group? Has the preliminary research been completed? Are the group members sufficiently prepared to discuss the topic? Is there a need for prework, reading, or special reports? Perhaps the item could be submitted to an ad hoc or standing group for further study prior to the full-group meeting. Is the desired outcome clear and written in a neutral tone? The agenda can also be set to get participants involved right away, so they come on time.

- *Decide how long the meeting needs to last to complete the desired outcome.* Determine how many items can be accommodated if the group has previously set a preferred length of time for the meeting.

- *Identify items by category* (information items, discussion items, action items) and cluster topics that are similar.

- *Carefully sequence the agenda items.*
  - Teams or boards that have many decisions to make often begin with a group of consent agenda items. These items are generally more routine in nature and do not require significant discussion. Group a number of action items together for efficiency, but make sure members have the background they need to make a decision on these items as a whole so the vote can be taken quickly at the meeting's outset.
  - The consent agenda includes items such as approval of the minutes of the last meeting.
  - Identify a few items that will help members work together as a group before they face more complex items.
  - Position more important items earlier in the meeting when members are better able to concentrate and be creative. Placing these items toward the beginning also helps in case some members have to leave early or you run out of time later in the meeting for items that need lengthy discussion.
  - Since you want the group to end on a unifying note, move more controversial items to an earlier place on the agenda. Some groups are tempted to put all action items at the end of the meeting, following all of the information sharing and information processing. Doing so puts pressure on the team and may reduce the quality of the dialogue if time becomes short.

- *Prepare a draft of the agenda.* Balance information sharing, discussion, and action items. If information and discussion items are related to an action item, place them together.

- *Send a copy of the agenda to every member of the group prior to the meeting.* Some groups prefer to have the agenda 24 or 48 hours prior to the meeting, and others determine the agenda at the close of the previous meeting. You may also want to make the agenda available to all constituencies by putting it in mailboxes, posting it on bulletin boards, or including it in a weekly bulletin. Include documentation that will help you achieve the meeting goals, such as reports, data, or prework that attendees should complete before the meeting.

- *Include opportunities for learning in the agenda.* As people contribute their expertise, provide opportunities for participants to take home new knowledge to benefit and add value to their own work. Provide an opportunity for members to engage in their own professional development as well as to accomplish the group's desired outcome.

- *Review the agenda-building process and the agenda formats occasionally to make sure the process continues to meet the needs of the group.*

ARRANGE THE FACILITY

Creating a proper atmosphere is as important for a meeting as it is in entertaining. The room environment and level of comfort will affect everyone's attitude toward the meeting. It is important to carefully consider the arrangements in advance and create a welcoming, positive atmosphere for an environment conducive to working.

I remember facilitating one meeting in which the afternoon sun shone directly into some group members' eyes and the window shades were broken. At another meeting, participants brought their coats because the room was known to have a faulty heating system. In these cases, it was hard for some individuals to focus on the work. Group members are better able to pay attention and participate when they have their physical needs met. Set a tone for the meeting by carefully attending to the following aspects.

Select a Meeting Room

Considerations such as which day and time and the length and number of times the group will meet will affect your choice of meeting space. Humans are creatures of habit, so it is best to try to meet in the same location, if not always at the same time or on a routine day. That means planning ahead to reserve your space.

If members of the group represent a variety of interests, however, such as a number of different schools, it may be beneficial to rotate the meeting location and have various members host the group. Doing so reminds members of the people whom the work may affect and varies the interest for participants, which can encourage them to attend. In fact, spending a few minutes learning about the location can be a positive experience for group members.

Another main consideration is the group's size. Most rooms will accommodate a group of 12 without too much trouble. It is better to have too much space than to be crowded, so if you have a choice, opt for the larger setting. Consider whether all the participants will be able to see each other, the facilitator, and any speakers who may be invited.

Tip: If you have too large a space, create artificial barriers to help the group fit the room. It helps to select a room that has furniture that can be easily moved.

Also make sure the room will be able to accommodate the work you have planned. For example, if you want to have the larger group break up into smaller groups, choose a setting in which you can set up in advance for both situations. You may want a room that will accommodate a single large group as well as several small groups working simultaneously.

Study the Room

If possible, spend a few minutes in the meeting room in advance of the meeting day so you have time to think about and plan the room arrangement. Check to be sure you know about aspects of the room that will affect the group's comfort level. The room will also influence the processes and large- or small-group structures that you can use during the meeting. Be sure to know the following:

Room

- Is the size of the room adequate for the different kinds of work you may do and the size of the group?
- Who will open the room? Who has a key?
- Where are the light switches?
- Where are the room temperature controls?
- What is the usual room temperature? Will the room need to be warmed or cooled in advance?
- Where is the nearest building entrance?
- Is the lighting adequate?
- Are there pillars or other things that could block group members' views?
- Is there room for a refreshment area?
- How many tables are in the room, and what shape are they?
- Are there enough chairs?
- Can the furniture be easily moved? Who will arrange it?
- Is there adequate wall space for hanging charts?
- Do you have permission to tape or pin notes to the wall?
- Do windows have shades or other means of controlling the light?
- Is the room located away from high-traffic areas?

Equipment

- Is there a screen?
- Where are the electrical outlets? What power cords will be needed?
- Is there a phone? Is there Internet access?
- Is there a microphone system?
- Is there a SMART board, an LCD projector, or multimedia equipment?
- Are there tables for the equipment, for the refreshments, for the materials, and for the facilitator?
- What other equipment or furniture might be needed?

Use Handout 1.9: Meeting Room Checklist to help you plan and to make notes after the meeting to improve future work.

Plan the Room Arrangement

Consider the size of the group and the purpose of the meeting. Will group members take notes? They will need tables. Will you work in one group, small groups, or both? Set up separate small-group work areas in advance so participants can move without having to rearrange the furniture. If you want to encourage discussion and dialogue, make sure all participants can see each other clearly.

The way you arrange the room and the tables sends clear messages the instant participants walk in. One square table at the front of the room signals that control resides there. A circle of chairs suggests an informal discussion without any note taking, which might imply little follow-up. Once you've considered your purpose and what the facility can accommodate, make the best arrangement you can.

Possible arrangements (see Figure 1.2) are as follows:

- *Boardroom.* Participants all sit around one large rectangular table. Use this setup with a smaller group who can fit at the table size available, generally 12 or fewer participants. This is a good arrangement for small meetings. The facilitator can work well and be seen from the front of the room. Disadvantages include a limit to the number of people who can be seated at the table, and the shape may imply a certain hierarchy.

- *Hollow Square.* Participants sit on the outside of several rectangular tables that form a square. A hollow square is useful when the only additional visual aid is a chart stand. A larger number of participants can fit in this shape, but it creates more distance between participants, and between participants and the facilitator or group leader.

- *U-Shaped.* Three rectangular tables are used to form a U shape. This setup is desirable when information will be visually recorded, displayed, and used during the meeting. It is convenient for groups of

HANDOUT 1.9: MEETING ROOM CHECKLIST

1. **Physical Arrangement**   Notes:
   - Temperature   _____
   - Heating/Cooling control (manual or locked)   _____
   - Entrance   _____
   - Registration area   _____
   - Lighting   _____
   - Screen   _____
   - Electrical outlets, power strips   _____
   - Refreshment area   _____
   - Tables   _____
   - Chairs   _____
   - Phone(s)   _____
   - Wall space   _____
   - Windows and window shades   _____
   - Size of room   _____
   - Partitioning   _____
   - Types of tables   _____
   - Possibilities for seating arrangements   _____

2. **Atmosphere**
   - Temperature   _____
   - Refreshments   _____
   - Lighting   _____
   - Restrooms   _____
   - Comfort of chairs   _____

3. **Audio/Visual**
   - Television   _____
   - VCR   _____
   - Overhead projector   _____
   - Screen   _____
   - Slide projector   _____
   - Laptop computer, projector   _____
   - Chart paper or Post-It chart paper if tape cannot be used _____
   - Markers, masking tape   _____

4. **Resource Materials**
   - Welcome sign   _____
   - Nametags/name plates   _____
   - Paper, pens, pencils   _____
   - Minutes from previous meeting   _____
   - List of participants   _____
   - Sign-in roster, reimbursement forms   _____
   - Sample documents, reports, data, background papers _____
   - Working papers of the group   _____
   - Menu for ordering lunch   _____

up to 20 or so and makes it easy for all to see the leader or facilitator. Participants also are able to see each other. The size of the table may make it less conducive to small-group discussion. The leader or facilitator's movement is limited, and the facilitator is perceived in a power position in a room with this setup. Chairs can be placed on the inside of the U if the group will work in small groups during the meeting.

• *Rounds.* All the participants are seated in small groups at round tables. This is a good arrangement for building a sense of being a team and for encouraging discussion. The leader or facilitator has more freedom as far as where he or she is positioned. A disadvantage is that it may encourage casual discussion, perhaps at inopportune times. Having more round tables also requires a larger room to allow for movement.

• *Herringbone (or V).* All participants are seated in small groups at tables of approximately six, so everyone at the table can see the screen and the facilitator or presenter. The advantage of this setup is the visual access and the table grouping that allows for small-group work and supports conversation.

> **Tip:** If someone else will be responsible for arranging the room, give that person a diagram.

Create a Positive Atmosphere

When the main form for seating has been settled, consider the many finer points of the room's setting. Remember to monitor the room environment when you meet.

Lights

Watch for flickering light bulbs or direct sunlight in people's faces, which can create irritability or cause headaches.

Temperature

Be sure the room temperature is adjusted appropriately prior to the meeting. Stay aware of the room temperature as the group meets. When individuals are too warm or too cold, energy drops.

Refreshments

Serve refreshments that heighten rather than "zap" energy. Provide high-protein foods, fruit, juice, nuts, water, and both caffeinated and decaffeinated drinks.

> **Tip:** Begin with too few seats rather than too many. Seats can be added if necessary, but empty chairs can become black holes of energy.

Comfort

Let members know the location of the restrooms. Face chairs away from doors and windows when possible.

Figure 1.2   Room Arrangements

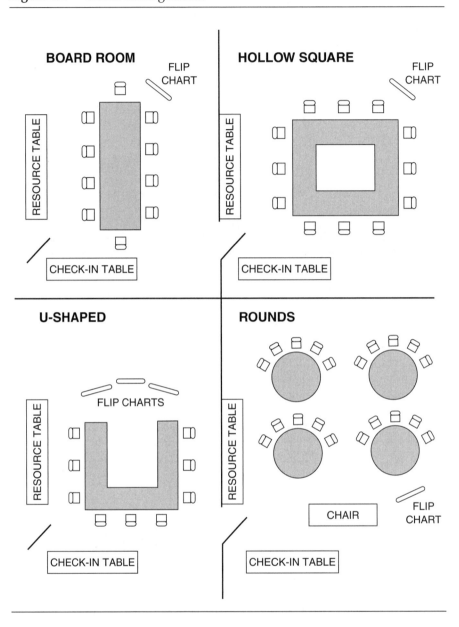

Gather Equipment and Supplies

Check equipment in advance and know who is available to help if equipment fails or you need additional supplies. Consider what supplies you will need, where you will get them, where you will place them in the room, and who is responsible for bringing the equipment and supplies to the meeting.

Equipment may include the following:

- Television or monitor
- VCR

- Overhead projector
- Screen(s) depending on the size of the room
- Laptop computer, LCD projector, mouse, remote control
- Chart paper
- Tape, pins, markers (use water-soluble markers to reduce odors in the room)
- Extension cords, power strips

The following are some supplies that might benefit the group's work:

- Registration materials
  - Welcome sign
  - Nametags or nameplates
  - Paper, pens, pencils
  - Reimbursement forms
  - University or district credit forms
  - Sign-in roster
  - Menu for ordering lunch
  - List of participants

- Materials for the meeting
  - Agenda
  - Background papers
  - Documents, reports
  - Data that will guide the work of the group
  - Working papers of the group
  - Minutes from previous meetings
  - Articles of interest
  - Books, reference materials

- Refreshments

While it may seem to some that several of these preparatory steps could be shortened or even skipped, they are essential components of the group's success. Someone told me recently that her group didn't need an agenda because members just came in and got to work. After a pause, I congratulated her, then asked her what the group's purpose was and if members ever spent time reflecting on what they had accomplished. Without any hesitation, she said the group didn't have any time for that—they had so much work, they had spent the last year just trying to get to the end, and they still hadn't gotten there.

Without a formalized structure and attention to the details outlined here, the work and the team relationships ultimately suffer. Members can't commit as fully to even attending the meeting if they don't clearly understand their purpose for being there. We all want to know what to expect when we walk into a meeting. We want to know when it will begin, something about the work we will be doing there, and what time we will end. A well-constructed agenda is a roadmap for the work ahead.

We want to be physically comfortable. We want a place to work that is not too cold or overly heated. Like our students, we want to be able to see the board/screen. And we want to know that the right people are in the room to do the work that needs to be done.

Setting up each of these components takes time. The time is better spent up front, before the group actually meets, than in trying to resolve issues that may arise later from a lack of preparation. It is always better to put in the extra preparation time attending to details. That is the difference between a meeting that works and one that falls apart, and between a team that achieves its desired outcome and a group that can't get past discussion.

Preparation is the first key to successful group work. The next key is knowing how to run the meeting well.

2

Getting the Group Started

I t is 3:55 p.m., and the school's hallways are clear. Two teachers enter the lounge area and grab bottles of water before taking their places at a large round meeting table. They greet one another, then pull notebooks and articles from their canvas bags, putting the papers neatly in front of them. As others file in, the teachers are focused on what they have read, highlighted, and made notes on in the margins. Other staff members join them and take seats around the table. The meeting begins promptly at 4 p.m.

The recorder calls the group's attention to the minutes of the last meeting, which had been included in their packets of materials, and asks for any changes.

After reviewing the agenda, the facilitator opens with a warm-up activity that renews relationships and sets the stage for the work at hand. One group member summarizes what she found important in the reading material. Other members join in, adding points and comparing their understandings. A veteran teacher who hasn't spoken yet volunteers to summarize. She also shares an example of how she used the information from the readings during the past week, changing her approach in working with an underachieving student.

The first-year teacher quietly calls the group's attention to the time limit stated on the agenda. Group members agree to return to several ideas from the readings in the next week, via e-mail or face-to-face.

Following the sequence of items on the agenda, the facilitator announces the next topic, and the science teacher goes to the flip chart and finds the page where the group had already begun a list. After quickly reviewing the items, the science teacher scribes the ideas that group members add to the list.

After completing the brainstorming and clarifying items, the group settles in to work, talking about how they can apply key ideas to change their own practices. Throughout the discussion, the members' commitment to the work and each other is evident in comments such as "I think what Carmen is saying is . . ." and "I like Fred's idea. I think we can take it even further by . . ." Fred's idea has sparked a discussion between a couple of members about their frustration with a particular student. They spend several minutes complaining, until another group member says, "I think we agreed to a meeting norm that says we won't try to solve individual problems." The conversation shifts back to the group's work.

Groups that work this smoothly aren't created. They develop. Robert Garmston (2005b) states,

> For school groups to get work done effectively, with minimum time and maximum results with maximum member engagement and satisfaction, members must learn specific concepts and skills. Groups need information about group member responsibilities and skills, agenda design, how to maintain focus in meetings, and how to keep decision-making authority clear. (p. 65)

Before the group can efficiently use processes that enable it to reach its goals, there must be ground rules. The roles need to be clearly defined, expectations shared, and any limits to the group's decision-making authority understood.

SET THE NORMS

Just as teachers in the classroom set rules, adults in meetings can set expectations for how the group will function. When the meetings run well, the group is able to focus on the task at hand, use time effectively, and accomplish the goals. *Norms* are the ground rules that groups set to guide the work of a group.

Beginning with a discussion of group members' expectations reveals preferences and experiences so that an agreement on the norms can be made. When all group members understand and share expected rules of behavior, the group functions more efficiently. Establishing shared ground rules and values that spell out the expectations and skills team members need is one characteristic of effective teams (Garmston & Wellman, 1999).

Identifying ground rules can also help ensure that all members are recognized and have an opportunity to be heard. Pat Roy, a consultant and former president of the National Staff Development Council (NSDC), says having the group begin by writing its own ground rules helps democratize a group, sparking discussions that allow each member to be heard (Richardson, 1999).

Provide Background

The first step in beginning to set norms with the group is to be sure members understand the rationale for doing so. Explain that the ground rules will help to

- ensure all individuals have the opportunity to contribute in the meeting;
- increase team productivity and effectiveness;
- facilitate the group's ability to achieve its goals; and
- encourage "good behavior" in every meeting.

The next step is for the group members to develop their own rules. There are many ways to facilitate this activity. One way is to share examples that other groups have developed. Another way is to ask group members to think about meetings they look forward to attending. Help them to identify and purposefully set out the expectations that will create that kind of meeting.

Understanding how these rules will be used is the next step. Guidelines for using ground rules are often helpful. The group may want to discuss and agree on what members will do with their ground rules. Ideas include the following:

- *We will create them as a team and reach consensus to adopt them.* By writing norms as a group, members build the capacity for honest discussion and feel more ownership. The consensus process ensures that all members have the opportunity to be heard.

- *We will review them at the beginning of each meeting.* A quick review of the norms reminds members what they agreed to do and helps renew their commitment to the agreement.

- *We will post them during all meetings and pay attention to them.* A visual display can be a useful reminder. "Simply writing norms does not guarantee that the group will remember and respect them," writes Joan Richardson (1999, p. 2).

- *We will commit to confronting behaviors that violate the norms.* The facilitator or group leader alone is not solely responsible for reminding a group member whose behavior is outside the established ground rules of the agreement. Robert Garmston (2002a) says the most effective groups' members understand that the group belongs to members, not leaders: "Group behavior is an aggregate of the choices of individuals. Groups sanction their members' actions and define acceptable and nonacceptable behaviors. Whether or not a group knows it is directing its own dynamics, this is the most determining factor in accomplishing work" (p. 76).

- *We will revise them when a need is identified.* Do not expect that new members will merely adopt the existing group rules. Each time a new group member is added, it is important to reestablish consensus around the ground rules.

• *We will evaluate how well our behavior aligned with our ground rules at the end of each meeting.* "Most groups have more work to do than they have time, yet the only way to improve is through reflection," says Garmston (2005a, p. 66). A few minutes spent reviewing whether members' actions demonstrated commitment to the ground rules can strengthen group trust and communication.

• *We will trust our group's wisdom in establishing the ground rules we need to ensure success.* The collective nature of the assembled group virtually guarantees that the knowledge and skills needed to establish an exemplary set of ground rules will be present. The key is trusting in that collective wisdom.

Determine whether the group can support the guidelines before adopting ground rules.

Agree on the Group's Ground Rules

After understanding what ground rules are and the rationale for specifying them and discussing how they are used, the group is ready to agree on its own set of ground rules.

Review the following samples of ground rules or group norms:

1. Start on time.

2. Develop and review the agenda.

3. Conduct one piece of business at a time.

4. Participation is a right *and* a responsibility.

5. Initiate ideas.

6. Support. Challenge. Counter. Differences resolved constructively lead to creative problem solving.

7. Give others a chance to talk. Silence does not always mean agreement.

8. Communicate authentically. What people say should reflect what they think as well as what they feel.

9. Conduct group business in front of the group.

10. Conduct personal business outside of the meeting.

11. Develop conditions of respect, acceptance, trust, and caring.

12. Develop alternative approaches to the solution of a problem.

13. Test for readiness to make decisions.

14. Assign follow-up actions and responsibilities.

15. Summarize what has been accomplished.

16. End on time.

SOURCE: From *Building Systems for Professional Growth: An Action Guide*, by Margaret A. Arbuckle and Lynn B. Murray, Regional Laboratory for Educational Improvement of the Northeast & Islands, 1989. Copyright by WestEd. Reprinted with permission of WestEd, www.wested.org.

These ground rules were developed by a national work team:

- Draw someone out who is quiet.
- Use an external facilitator when necessary.
- Balance quality and task orientation.
- Use conflict-reducing strategies.
  - Ask for clarification.
  - Seek underlying assumptions.
  - Display disagreements with ideas, not individuals.

- Balance business and community.
- Strive for conciseness (self-monitoring).
- Listen actively and avoid side conversations.
- Avoid repetition.
- Use frequent consensus checks.
- Help the leader keep people on subject.
- Establish a friendly, humorous signal for off-task conversation.
- Share roles of facilitator, scribe, recorder, timekeeper, and process guide.
- Contribute to personal/professional sharing opportunities.
- Feel comfortable expressing anger.
- Display courtesy and respect for all members.
- Use appropriate, constructive, timely humor.
- Listen actively.
- Avoid cliques—make personal contacts.

A leadership team created these ground norms and operating procedures:

Norms

- Start and end on time.
- Keep meetings open.
- Differentiate between brainstorming and discussion.
- Address only schoolwide issues.
- Express disagreement with ideas, not with individuals.
- Feel responsible to express differing opinions within the meeting.
- Maintain confidentiality regarding disagreements expressed during the meeting.
- Reach decisions by consensus.

Operating Procedures

- Meet only when there is a meaningful agenda.
- Expect a leadership team member to make a commitment for one year.
- Have a different facilitator and recorder for each meeting.

After examining the samples of the norms from other groups, ask members to silently and individually make a list of the characteristics of effective meetings they have experienced.

After a few minutes, ask group members to share their lists and discuss whether any characteristics of effective meetings can be stated as a ground rule. If the group is large, this discussion may be completed more effectively by breaking up into smaller discussion groups.

Next, depending on the size of the group, have individuals or small groups prepare a list of five or six ground rules. Ground rules can help to answer questions in these categories about how the group decides to function:

- *Time.* Will we set a beginning and ending time? Will we start and end on time?

- *Listening.* How will we encourage listening? How will we discourage interrupting? What agreements will this group make regarding active listening? How will we ensure active participation? Do we need to discuss the need for openness? Are there any behaviors that could interfere with active listening (grading papers, working on e-mail on a personal handheld device, knitting, or cutting out letters, etc.)? Invite the group to discuss what it means to listen actively and make agreements about what is and is not acceptable.

- *Confidentiality.* Will the meetings be open? Will what we say in the meeting be held in confidence? What can be said after the meeting? Are minutes shared with members, or are they shared broadly? How much detail is shared about the process and the agreements or disagreements on the way to a decision?

- *Decision Making.* How will we make decisions? Are we an advisory or a decision-making body? What format for decision making will we use? (See Chapter 4 for ideas about group decision making.) What processes will we use? How will we deal with conflict? Is it important for this group to discuss the acceptability of disagreement during the process? How will this group use data to improve the quality of all decisions?

- *Expectations.* What do we expect from members? How will the group share the workload? Who is responsible for what tasks? Will we have an attendance policy? How will we encourage everyone's participation?

- *Power/Authority/Influence.* How will we address power, authority, and influence issues? What will the relationships be between and among the principal, teachers, parents, and others? Are team members part of a formal hierarchy, or do all members of the team have an equal voice in the decision-making process?

- *Team Development.* How will this group learn together? Are members committed to continuous learning? How will you set priorities for your team learning?

- *Other.* Are there other processes this group wants to address? Are there issues unique to this group?

When the group has had about 15 minutes to talk about and identify some ideas for its own ground rules, begin recording members' ideas on chart paper. If the group is divided into small groups, ask a representative from each to present the smaller groups' recommendations. Identify similar recommendations and begin the discussion with these. Continue discussing the ideas until the group has made choices, understood, and agreed to the language they will use to state their norms.

Establish ground rules early in the group's formation. Groups who have not established ground rules have no agreement to reference. When they do not function well, they can return to the process and write ground rules, but it is harder to break habits than to return to expectations that were built on group consensus. And even when they have set initial norms, groups can always revise them if they need to as they learn to work together.

> **Tip:** You may wish to display the group's final set of norms. Remember, however, that ground rules are open to revision. Some groups find that listing them on the backs of name tents makes them personal and available for easy reference.

It is important to trust the group to set the norms that it needs. One group set norms including, "We will talk in 30-second sound bites," and "We will not restate comments that have already been made." That group clearly understood their weakness was talking too much and set norms to reduce their negative behavior.

Here is an example of an interactive way to review the ground rules and promote shared ownership if the group has already agreed to review the ground rules at the start of every meeting. During a meeting of the NSDC, the NSDC president assigned each board member one of the group's norms before the start of a meeting and outlined an exercise to remind the group of the ground rules. One exercise might be having each board member take a turn describing what the norm looks and sounds like in action. Other group members try to guess and name the ground rule being described. The description stops when a member guesses correctly. Beginning the meeting this way reminds the group of the rules members have agreed will govern their behavior. It also provides a transition time before the group begins that meeting's specific work.

Also see Handout 2.1: Developing Norms and Handout 2.2: Norms of the NSDC Board of Trustees.

Determine Operating Procedures

After developing ground rules, the team may also decide on operating procedures. It is important to make decisions about each of the procedures. The following topics and questions will guide your planning and clarify expectations.

- *Meetings.* How frequently will we meet? Where will we meet? When will the meetings begin and end? How long will the meetings last? Can meetings be extended or shortened? Who will decide? Who can cancel meetings? Is it acceptable to call emergency meetings?

- *Minutes.* What format will be used to present the minutes? To whom and how will minutes be distributed? What is the process for amending and approving minutes as public record?

(Text continues on page 45)

HANDOUT 2.1: DEVELOPING NORMS

Comments to the Facilitator

This activity will enable a group to develop a set of operating norms or ground rules. In existing groups, anonymity will help ensure that everyone is able to express their ideas freely. That is the reason for suggesting that the facilitator provide pens or pencils and ask that everyone use the same type of writing instrument.

Directions

1. Indicate to the group that effective groups generally have a set of norms that governs individual behavior, facilitates the work of the group, and enables the group to accomplish its task.

2. Provide examples of norms.

3. Recommend to the group that it establish a set of norms
    *   to ensure that all individuals have the opportunity to contribute in the meeting;
    *   to increase productivity and effectiveness; and
    *   to facilitate the achievement of its goals.

4. Give five index cards and the same kind of writing tool to each person in the group.

5. Ask each person to reflect on and record behaviors they consider ideal behaviors for a group. Ask them to write one idea on each of their cards.

6. The facilitator should shuffle all the cards together. Every effort should be made to provide anonymity for individuals, especially if the group has worked together before.

7. Turn cards face up and read each card aloud. Allow time for the group members to discuss each idea. Tape or tack each card to a display board so that all group members can see it. As each subsequent card is read aloud, ask the group to determine if it is similar to another idea that already has been expressed. Cards with similar ideas should be grouped together.

8. When all of the cards have been sorted into groups, ask the group to write the norm suggested by that group of cards. Have one group member record these new norms on a large sheet of paper.

9. Review the proposed norms with the group. Determine whether the group can support the norms before the group adopts them.

When Establishing Norms, Consider	Proposed Norm
Time • When will the meeting begin and end? • Will the meeting begin and end on time?	
Communication Style/Active Listening • What agreements will this group make regarding active listening? • How will we discourage interruptions? • What are our expectations about cell phone/laptop/PDA use?	
Confidentiality/Open Communication • Will the meetings be open? • Is there a need to maintain confidentiality? • How will we share information after the meeting?	
Decision Making • How will we make decisions? • Are we an advisory or a decision-making body? • Will we reach decisions by consensus? • What processes will we use? • How will this group use data?	
Participation/Workload/Expectations • What do we expect from members? • What is our expectation about everyone's participation? • How will the group share the workload? • "Who" is responsible for "what"? • How will we recognize and accommodate style differences?	
Power/Authority • How will we work with the power, authority, and influence of some members of the team? • What will the relationships be between and among the members?	
Team Development • How will this group learn together? • Is there a commitment to continuous learning?	
Conflict Resolution • How will we resolve our differences? • Is it important for this group to discuss the acceptability of disagreement during the process?	

SOURCE: Adapted from *Tools for Change Workshops*, Oxford, OH: National Staff Development Council, 1993, and reprinted from *Tools for Schools*, August/September 1999.

HANDOUT 2.2: NORMS OF THE NSDC BOARD OF TRUSTEES

- Trustees ensure that they are fully present by preparing for the meeting and attending to factors that affect their physical and mental engagement.

- Trustees listen carefully to each other, and everyone's contributions are invited and welcomed.

- Trustees are responsible for examining all points of view before consensus is reached.

- Trustees are involved to their level of comfort. Each person is responsible for airing his or her views during the meeting rather than discussing them in other settings.

- The Board accomplishes its tasks in a collegial and friendly way.

- The Board welcomes appropriate humor because it helps Trustees work effectively together.

- The Board holds discussions, comments, and deliberations in confidence.

Principles

- The Board of Trustees functions as a *community*, operating by consensus rather than majority rule.

- The basis for Board policy making is the NSDC strategic plan.

SOURCE: Provided by the NSDC Board of Trustees, 2006.

- *Agenda.* Who prepares the agenda? How do participants/others influence the agenda? How are emergency items/new business/surprises handled? How do members get advanced notice of agenda? How far ahead are agendas distributed? Who gets a copy of the agenda? When are minutes distributed?

- *Visitors/Alternates.* Are observers welcome? Who may address the team? What are the procedures for addressing the group? What is the role of alternates/substitutes on the team? Is it acceptable for group members to extend invitations to others to meet with the team? Who has the right to do this? What process do team members use to request information or authorization?

- *Resources.* What resources are available to the group? What resources are available to subcommittees? How are decisions made about using group resources? What information is available to all members?

- *Sharing Responsibilities.* What duties can be rotated or shared? Will participants share duties? If so, how? What processes will be used to encourage ownership and commitment to the project and the work?

- *Other Issues.* What other key agreements need to be made by this group to work effectively together?

> **Tip:** Start an operating-procedures manual so ground rules and processes can be easily transferred to the next leaders of the group.

When the group has worked through several meetings using its new ground rules, a helpful check up to keep members aware is provided on Handout 2.3: Measuring Collaborative Norms.

ESTABLISH ROLES

Another strategy to help groups function smoothly is to assign or share a number of responsibilities among group members. Groups offer opportunities for members to play a variety of roles: roles that enable the group to function more smoothly and roles that help the group focus on its task.

Complete these steps to get the group started:

- *Review the Roles.* Have the group review or discuss each of the possible roles outlined below, including what qualities are helpful and the resources available for those fulfilling the responsibilities.

- *Identify Which Roles the Group Needs.* Not every group uses all the roles at every meeting. Group members should discuss which roles the group wants to use. The roles of agenda builder, facilitator, and recorder (minutes taker) routinely need to be filled for every meeting.

(Text continues on page 49)

HANDOUT 2.3: MEASURING COLLABORATIVE NORMS

Purpose

To surface staff or team members' awareness of the group's use of collaborative norms and to assist staff and team to identify areas in which the staff or team wants to focus.

Directions

1. Make enough copies of the inventory to allow each member to have his or her own copy.
2. Organize a large group into smaller groups of three persons each. Ask each group of three to rate the larger group's adherence to each norm from low to high. (Estimated Time: 20 minutes.)
3. At the conclusion, reassemble the larger group and invite one person from each small group to report out the responses. (Estimated Time: 30 minutes.)
4. Using the same scale, mark each group's response on a poster-size piece of paper.
5. Identify norms where the groups scored the lowest.
6. Invite the group to develop a plan to improve its abilities in those areas.

1. Pausing

⇦ **Low – – – – – – – – – – High** ⇨

The Norm: Pausing before responding or asking a question allows time for thinking and enhances dialogue, discussion, and decision making.

- Listens attentively to others' ideas with mind and body.
- Allows time for thought after asking question or making a response.
- Rewords in own mind what others are saying to further understand their communication.
- Waits until others have finished before entering the conversation.

2. Paraphrasing

⇦ **Low – – – – – – – – – – High** ⇨

The Norm: Using a paraphrase starter that is comfortable for you such as "So . . ." Or "As you are . . ." or "You're thinking . . ." and following the starter with a paraphrase assists members of a group to hear and understand each other as they formulate decisions.

- Uses paraphrases that acknowledge and clarify content and emotions.
- Uses paraphrases that summarize and organize.

- Uses paraphrases that shift a conversation to different levels of abstraction.
- Uses nonverbal communication in paraphrasing.

3. Probing

⇦ **Low** ‒ ‒ ‒ ‒ ‒ ‒ ‒ ‒ ‒ ‒ **High** ⇨

The Norm: Using gentle, open-ended probes or inquiries such as "Please say more . . ." or "I'm curious about . . ." or "I'd like to hear more about . . ." or "Then you are saying . . ."

- Increases the clarity and precision of the group's thinking.
- Seeks agreement on what words mean.
- Asks questions to clarify facts, ideas, stories.
- Asks questions to clarify explanations, implications, consequences.
- Asks questions to surface assumptions, points of view, beliefs, values.

4. Putting Ideas on the Table

⇦ **Low** ‒ ‒ ‒ ‒ ‒ ‒ ‒ ‒ ‒ ‒ **High** ⇨

The Norm: Ideas are the heart of a meaningful dialogue. Label the intention of your comments. For example, you might say, "Here is one idea . . ." or "One thought I have is . . ." or "Here is a possible approach."

- States intention of communication.
- Reveals all relevant information.
- Considers intended communication for relevance and appropriateness before speaking.
- Provides facts, inferences, ideas, opinions, suggestions.
- Explains reasons behind statements, questions, and actions.
- Removes or announces the modification of own ideas, opinions, points of view.

5. Paying Attention to Self and Others

⇦ **Low** ‒ ‒ ‒ ‒ ‒ ‒ ‒ ‒ ‒ ‒ **High** ⇨

The Norm: Meaningful dialogue is facilitated when each group member is conscious of self and of others and is aware of not only what he or she is saying but also how it is said and how others are responding. This includes paying attention to learning styles when planning for, facilitating and participating in group meetings. Responding to others in their own language forms is one manifestation of this norm.

(Continued)

Handout 2.3 (Continued)

- Maintains awareness of own thoughts and feelings while having them.
- Maintains awareness of others' voice patterns, nonverbal communications, and use of physical space.
- Maintains awareness of group's task, mood, and relevance of own and others' contributions.

6. Presuming Positive Presuppositions

⇦ **Low — — — — — — — — — High** ⇨

The Norm: Assuming that others' intentions are positive promotes and facilitates meaningful dialogue and eliminates unintentional put-downs. Using positive presuppositions in your speech is one manifestation of this norm.

- Acts as if others mean well.
- Restrains impulsivity triggered by own emotional responses.
- Uses positive presuppositions when responding to and inquiring of others.

7. Pursuing a Balance Between Advocacy and Inquiry

⇦ **Low — — — — — — — — — High** ⇨

The Norm: Pursuing and maintaining a balance between advocating a position and inquiring about one's own and others' positions assists the group to become a learning organization.

- Advocates for own ideas and inquires into the ideas of others.
- Acts to provide equitable opportunities for participation.
- Presents rationale for positions, including assumptions, facts, and feelings.
- Disagrees respectfully and openly with ideas and offers rationale for disagreement.
- Inquires of others about their reasons for reaching and occupying a position.

SOURCE: Reprinted with permission from *The Adaptive School: A Sourcebook for Developing Collaborative Groups*, Norwood, MA: Christopher-Gordon, 1999, and reprinted from *Tools for Schools*, October/November, 2002.

• *Decide How Long Members Will Fill Each Role.* When the group is ongoing, roles are often set for periods of time. Some groups have members fill roles meeting by meeting or month by month; others have a member take one role for 6 or 12 months. If the group is shorter-lived, one member might take on a specific role for the duration of the group's activities. Sharing roles among team members helps the group function with a higher level of trust, as each member has opportunities to learn new skills. Teams might want to establish a process for sharing responsibilities. Some people mentor one another in a specific role to get support and practice. The best way to learn the skills related to these roles is to perform the role.

• *Select Members' Roles.* For the first meeting, the group chairperson or facilitator often assigns roles. For subsequent meetings, ask for volunteers to take responsibility for each role the group has decided to use. Encourage all to participate. Be aware of the symbolism of who fills the assignments. For example, if teachers take all the leadership roles on a shared decision-making team involving the community, parents might feel excluded. If the administrator takes on the role of the primary facilitator, traditional roles might continue. Some groups have a designated leader, that is, a person who has an external position with a title, such as principal, department head, grade-level chair, or curriculum coordinator. When a team leader serves as the facilitator, traditional roles may be reinforced. Review the responsibilities of the group roles and decide how to divide the workload.

The following are roles for the group to discuss and decide whether or not to use. Typical roles are group member, facilitator, timekeeper, recorder, scribe, agenda builder, and process observer. For each role, there is a job description, including qualities needed for the role, how to play the role, common responsibilities, and when the role is needed.

In addition, every member of the group plays a role as a group member, encouraging each other and participating in a productive, meaningful way to accomplish the group's work.

The Group Member

The Role. The most important role in any group is that of group member. The substance of conversation comes from the group. The work of the group belongs to all its members, and it is members' responsibility to make sure meetings are effective.

Qualities. Members of effective groups agree to come to meetings prepared, complete assignments, and actively participate in the group's work. When members are willing to ask questions, challenge assumptions, seek clarity, and move the group forward on issues, groups are more likely to accomplish these goals. In effective groups, members give the group their undivided attention. They take the roles they agree to and prepare themselves for the tasks assigned to those roles, often reviewing the resources available and reflecting on how well they performed those tasks in meetings.

How To. Being a positive member of the group involves seeking information in an open and nonthreatening manner; offering opinions as opinions, not as facts; energizing the group, when necessary; using appropriate decision-making and problem-solving skills; seeking agreement; committing to fairness, openness, and respect toward other group members; and acknowledging others' contributions. Good group members respect time constraints, honor others' knowledge and value their contributions, focus their disagreements on issues rather than individuals, and are active participants. They come to the meeting willing to focus on the work at hand. They turn off personal digital assistants (PDAs) and cell phones. In high-functioning groups, members often spend time reflecting on their responsibilities to the group.

Team Member Responsibilities

- Come prepared to meetings
- Complete assignments in a timely manner
- Develop the agenda in an open and systematic manner
- Initiate an agenda item in a way that opens discussion
- Seek information in an open and nonthreatening manner
- Give information that contributes to the knowledge and decision-making process
- Offer opinions as opinions, not as facts
- Elaborate on another's contribution
- Combine ideas from two or more participants into one stronger idea
- Energize the group, when necessary
- Use different decision-making and problem-solving strategies as appropriate
- Seek consensus
- Encourage participation from all members
- Find common ground between contrary opinions
- Give and be open to feedback on the impact of various types of behavior and the impact on the group
- Remind the group of its commitments to fairness, openness, and respect
- Ask to examine group effectiveness at key intervals
- Acknowledge individuals' contributions to the group

Resources. For a quick check of how well members function as part of the group, see Handout 2.4: Who Does What In Our Group? and Handout 2.5: Rate Yourself as a Team Player.

(Text continues on page 54)

HANDOUT 2.4: WHO DOES WHAT IN OUR GROUP?

Below is a list and a brief description of different roles and functions that people play in groups. First, assess your own behavior by indicating how often you perform each role (1 = rarely; 5 = all the time). Then choose the one person in the group who best fits each role description and write that person's name next to the role.

		Me	*Others*
1.	*Initiator/Contributor.* Proposes goals, ideas, solutions; defines problems; suggests procedures.		
2.	*Information and Opinion Seeker.* Asks for clarification and suggestions; looks for facts and feelings; solicits ideas and values of other members.		
3.	*Information Giver.* Offers facts and relevant information or experience.		
4.	*Opinion Giver.* States beliefs about alternatives; focuses on values rather than facts.		
5.	*Clarifier/Elaborator.* Interprets; gives examples; defines terms; clears up confusion or ambiguity.		
6.	*Coordinator/Summarizer.* Pulls ideas, opinions, and suggestions together; summarizes and restates; tries to draw members' activities together; offers conclusions.		
7.	*Gatekeeper/Expediter.* Keeps communication open among all members; opens up opportunities for others to participate.		
8.	*Harmonizer.* Tries to reduce conflict and tension; attempts to reconcile differences.		
9.	*Encourager.* Supportive of others; praises efforts and ideas; accepts contributions.		
10.	*Evaluator.* Helps group assess whether it has reached a conclusion.		

SOURCE: From *Building Systems for Professional Growth: An Action Guide,* by Margaret A. Arbuckle and Lynn B. Murray, Regional Laboratory for Educational Improvement of the Northeast & Islands, 1989. Copyright by WestEd. Reprinted with permission of WestEd, www.wested.org.

HANDOUT 2.5: RATE YOURSELF AS A TEAM PLAYER

Comments to the Facilitator

The facilitator should prepare individual sheets ahead of the team meeting and distribute to team members. Before distributing, tell them when results will be available and how results will be used.

Ensure anonymity for respondents by having team members fold their surveys and drop them into a box.

Calculate survey results privately and share the total results with the entire group publicly during the next team meeting.

Lead a discussion about possible implications of the responses. *In what areas is there already substantial agreement that the team is performing well together? What areas does this team need to work on? What are some strategies for improvement in that area?*

Directions

Effective school improvement teams are made up of individuals who respect each other and work well together. Your behavior has an enormous impact on the team's ability to do its work efficiently and effectively. The following is a series of questions about your behavior in your work group. Answer each question honestly. There are no right or wrong answers. Describe your behavior as accurately as possible.

1. I offer facts, opinions, ideas, suggestions, and relevant information during my team's discussions.

   Never   1   2   3   4   5   6   7   **Always**

2. I express my willingness to cooperate with other group members and my expectation that they will also be cooperative.

   Never   1   2   3   4   5   6   7   **Always**

3. I am open and candid in my dealings with the entire group.

   Never   1   2   3   4   5   6   7   **Always**

4. I support team members who are on the spot and struggling to express themselves.

   Never   1   2   3   4   5   6   7   **Always**

5. I take risks in expressing new ideas and current feelings during a team discussion.

   Never   **1**   **2**   **3**   **4**   **5**   **6**   **7**   **Always**

6. I communicate to other team members that I am aware of and appreciate their abilities, talents, capabilities, skills, and resources.

   Never   **1**   **2**   **3**   **4**   **5**   **6**   **7**   **Always**

7. I offer help and assistance to anyone on the team in order to improve the team's performance.

   Never   **1**   **2**   **3**   **4**   **5**   **6**   **7**   **Always**

8. I accept and support the openness of other team members, supporting them for taking risks and encouraging individuality.

   Never   **1**   **2**   **3**   **4**   **5**   **6**   **7**   **Always**

9. I share materials, books, sources of information, and other resources with team members in order to promote the success of all members and the team as a whole.

   Never   **1**   **2**   **3**   **4**   **5**   **6**   **7**   **Always**

10. Three things I might do to increase the effectiveness of our team include:

    1. _____

    2. _____

    3. _____

SOURCE: Adapted from the South Carolina State Department of Education and reprinted with permission from *Tools for Schools*, April/May 2001.

I remember one group in which a member was constantly antagonizing the others. He often began speaking by saying, "I don't mean to be the devil's advocate, but . . ." He didn't get his way, and so he just kept harping. A scribe can help in this situation by pointing out where the comment has been recorded. A good facilitator can assist (see Chapter 3). More important, however, is the role of other group members, who can exert the power of the group to have members observe the ground rules.

Set Expectations

Having all members understand and agree to meeting roles is one of Garmston's five principles of effective meetings (2002b). Establishing roles and deciding who will fill each is an important part of ensuring that the meeting is productive. Each role contributes a unique element of an efficient operation. Taking the time at the outset to set clear expectations will avoid the frustrations of meetings in which no one has performed the tasks assigned to these key roles.

When members understand their specific responsibilities and know their absence will affect the quality of the work, they are more likely to arrive ready to focus on the tasks at hand, and the group as a whole will accomplish more.

By setting clear expectations for how the group will perform through establishing ground rules and by outlining and assigning roles early on, groups can proceed to focus on the work itself. As Garmston notes (2002a), groups that have clear ground rules and clear roles are more able to avoid mistakes, make important decisions, and have productive meetings. The next piece in working toward the group's goal is developing the group's background knowledge.

The Facilitator

The Role. A facilitator helps the group achieve its desired outcome, working with group members to assess the group's needs, examine the issues, make decisions, and plan for action. Tom Kayser (1990, 1994) lists a host of responsibilities for the facilitator: managing the process during the group's session; coordinating the activities and dialogue required for the group to achieve the outcomes it desires; clarifying the issues, checking for understanding, and summarizing ideas for the group; and ensuring an appropriate balance between the task and the people. In addition, the facilitator is sometimes responsible for meeting details, such as arranging for a location, setting up the room, and following through on postmeeting assignments.

Qualities. Facilitators must be extremely organized to manage the group's details before and after the meeting. They must be individuals who follow through with tasks. During the meeting, a good facilitator is a good listener, someone with high-level communication skills, able to summarize and paraphrase thoughts and ideas and move a conversation ahead, and preferably with coaching skills, able to lead a group. Practice with building consensus in a group is extremely valuable.

How To. Determine who will serve as facilitator. Some options are having the chairperson also serve as the facilitator; asking one or two members of the group to serve as facilitator or cofacilitators; rotating the role among all members of the group, with volunteers signing up for each meeting; and asking a nonmember with strong facilitation skills to serve.

There are advantages and disadvantages to each option. Having the chairperson serve as the facilitator may reinforce a hierarchy and role power, particularly if the chairperson's role outside the group is one of authority. However, this person might also bring knowledge and experience to the role that would benefit the group. Having select individuals from the group can keep the role internal but limits the contributions these individuals can make while they are acting as facilitators. Rotating the role among all group members allows each person to grow in skill, but the quality of facilitation may differ with members' levels of ability in this role. Asking a nonmember to facilitate can bring in a person skilled in the job, but it may be difficult to find a volunteer. If the task is complex or time consuming, or if local participants would have difficulty being neutral, it can sometimes be helpful to hire a person from outside the group, someone with no vested interest in the group's work.

Facilitating is a complex, learned skill. If group members share the role, those with less experience may benefit from asking for the help of a mentor and using external resources, such as those included in the handouts for this chapter.

Ask group members to think about meetings they have attended in which facilitators were and were not used, and then discuss the facilitator's role and contributions to the success of the meeting. The group may list specific roles or responsibilities members want to assign the facilitator. A list of the facilitator's roles posted in the meeting can help the facilitator fill the role and meet the group's expectations.

Resources. Handout 2.6: Group Wise.

(Text continues on page 60)

HANDOUT 2.6: GROUP WISE

The Facilitator Is a Group's Instrument for Expressing and Understanding Relevant Ideas and Information

By Robert J. Garmston

Facilitating a meeting is hard work. It requires a clear sense of purpose, a juggler's gift of attending to everything at once, and a teacher's skill at supporting others in producing results. Exquisite facilitation is delicate, sensitive to individuals, the group, the goals, and the context in which the group works (Schwarz, 1994, p. 56).

In our work, a facilitator is (1) one who manages processes for a group so it can plan, problem-solve, share information, evaluate, and make decisions efficiently and effectively; and (2) one who improves group members' ability to work together effectively and helps groups improve their processes.

Because facilitators don't direct meeting content, some mistakenly believe the role is a passive one. Nothing could be further from the truth. The facilitator is the group's instrument for expressing and understanding relevant ideas and information. The facilitator supports the group in using diverse group resources, sound decision making, and effective problem solving.

A skilled facilitator knows the work belongs to the group, not the facilitator, and chooses words that distinguish the facilitator from group members. When one simultaneously serves as a facilitator and a working member of a group, this perspective calls for special resolve to remain neutral about content.

The Language of Facilitation

Learning to facilitate adult groups is often complicated by limited opportunities to practice. One approach to learning is to isolate, analyze, and practice skill subsets. Look at the list of purposes and write down phrases you typically use for each category. Then compare your list with the examples here for self-study. The examples are not "best" phrases and are certainly not the only ones that accomplish facilitation. They don't account for facilitator styles and context, but serve as a starting place for review.

Focusing

Be organized, be brief, and be specific. Use words and phrases that have one meaning. Tell the group what it is to do, why or how the purpose relates to the bigger context of their work, and the specific outcome to be achieved at each stage.

Review this language facilitators might use to:

1. **Get Attention**
   - Stop. Look this direction.
   - Please push the pause button.
   - Can everyone hear what John is saying?

2. **Clarify Purpose**
   - Today's task is to ____ (approve, generate, select, identify, explore, resolve).
   - There are three issues: What happened in the past, what you can do now, and what you can do in the future. Today's focus is what you can do now.
   - Today's intention is to build a foundation for the rest of your task. During this session, you will identify what you want to know on a staff survey and decide how you will use the data. We will not address writing survey questions today.

3. **Give Directions**
   - This morning you analyzed data. Now the task is to look for causal factors. Here is the first step . . .
   - As teams, identify some ideas you would like to explore. Prepare to share your two most important ideas.
   - The intention is to provide a forum to safely express your concerns. So, work with a neighbor and identify your most urgent concerns about the project.
   - This is a three-step process. First you will _____, then you will _____, and finally _____.

COMMON FACILITATION PURPOSES
Focus 1. Get attention. 2. Clarify purpose. 3. Give directions. **Engage** 4. Enlist participation. 5. Enlarge perspectives. 6. Invite group awareness. **Connect** 7. Foster understanding. 8. Promote agreements.

Engaging

In the following phrases, the language moves from prescriptive statements toward more interpretative comments. Important principles are using descriptive rather than evaluative words; assuming that individuals have valuable contributions and that if they feel psychologically safe they will share; giving people choices to empower them; using proper nouns rather than pronouns; providing scaffolds for people to examine issues from outside perspectives; and allowing for small group conversations to provide psychological safety.

(Continued)

Handout 2.6 (Continued)

Some things a facilitator might say to:

4. **Enlist Participation**
   - Here are some suggestions for how to get the most value out of today's meeting. One, please be responsible for your comfort and learning. Don't wait for a break to make yourself comfortable. Be responsible as well for your learning. If you can't hear someone, say, "Louder please"; if someone is speaking too abstractly and you need a concrete example, please ask for it.
   - If you disagree with an idea, let the group know. Use the phrase, "I see it a different way."
   - A lot of people want to comment. Let's line them up. Doris, you're first, Juanita will be second, Sam will follow Juanita. . . . Remember your numbers. OK, Doris, start us off.
   - What are your concerns regarding this topic? Take a moment and tell your neighbor.
   - Can we hear from someone who hasn't spoken?

5. **Enlarge Perspectives**
   - What patterns, categories, or themes do you see in this data?
   - You have identified a number of things you will see when students are successful. What might you hear?
   - What inferences, explanations, or conclusions might you draw?
   - To begin this conversation, let's brainstorm questions (or assumptions) about this initiative.

6. **Invite Group Awareness**
   - What's going on right now?
   - What does the group want to do?
   - The group seems to be stuck. Talk to your table group. Is there something important that's not being talked about?
   - You began this session talking about assessment. The last few comments have been about schedules. On which do you want to focus?
   - People seem tired. Do you want to take a break or do you want to push on for 15 minutes?
   - How is the group doing on its norm of listening to one another? Tell your partner.

Connecting

Terms like "some of," "hunches," "might," and "maybe" invite thinking while conveying that such thought is only exploratory. The language of connection becomes, at times, more artfully vague than the language of focus or engagement.

Some things a facilitator might say to:

7. **Foster Understanding**
   - Sid, could you paraphrase what Sally said? Sally, did he get it right? (If not . . .) Sally, say it again.
   - Can you say specifically what you mean by the term "accelerate"?

- It seems Antonio is advocating for doing this now, and Alice is recommending more time. Who can give us reasons supporting each position?
- Ellen, I think Eduardo is saying he wants to increase requirements for all students, not just the middle students. Is that right, Eduardo? Eduardo, do you understand what Ellen is saying?
- I think the group is clear about what you want to do, Aldo. What they are asking for is why. Can you help the group understand the reasons?

8. **Promote Agreements**
   - Are you ready for a decision?
   - What values will drive your decision-making processes?
   - OK, what are the different ideas you've heard? What solution might accommodate all of them?
   - It seems two positions are being expressed here. Would two people representing each be willing to form a subgroup and bring a recommendation back to the whole group?
   - I think I'm hearing agreement on that point. Can we do a quick thumbs check? Thumbs up, you agree. Down, you disagree. Sideways, you're not sure or don't care. (After seeing thumbs and one or two opposing the majority view: OK, help us understand your concerns with the proposition. What would need to be different for you to feel OK about it? Or: Is this a matter of preference or principle? Or: Are you willing to give it a try until the next reporting period?
   - Write your understandings of the group's decision. . . . Test it with a neighbor and edit if necessary. (Now hear some and help the group edit for accuracy.)

Enlarging Your Personal Repertoire

Pay attention to others' facilitation styles and language. Jot down phrases they use. Isolate language from one or two of the purposes above to practice. Jot down in advance phrases you would like to incorporate into your next facilitation. Practice facilitation phrases when working with students. Keep in mind that knowing is different from understanding. To understand, groups must explain, apply, or interpret information. Have these types of thinking be a focus for your facilitation outcomes.

Reference

Schwarz, R. (1994). *The skilled facilitator: Practical wisdom for developing effective groups.* San Francisco: Jossey-Bass.

SOURCE: Reprinted with permission from *JSD,* Spring 2003 (Vol. 24, No. 2).

The Facilitator's Roles and Responsibilities

- *Takes Neutral Role Position on All Issues.* The facilitator is not a formal member of the group, but rather a "servant leader" of the group. The facilitator does not advocate a position.
- *Focuses Energy of Group on the Agenda.* The facilitator keeps the group focused on the tasks to be accomplished at the meeting. The group can be focused with questions or statements such as "How does this relate to our objective?" or "We have strayed from our agenda and need to return to the issue of . . ."
- *Suggests Alternative Procedures in Problem-Solving Situations.* The facilitator proposes options when a process is not enabling the group to achieve its goal.
- *Protects Individuals From Verbal Attack.* The facilitator ensures that individuals are not attacked for expressing contrary opinions.
- *Encourages the Participation of All Members.* The facilitator ensures all members have equal opportunity to contribute and seeks opinions from quieter participants.
- *Keeps Enthusiasm High.* The facilitator shows interest in what's being said and uses "attending" behaviors.
- *Enables Win-Win Solutions.* The facilitator helps the group hear and respect all viewpoints and facilitates consensus or the will of the group.
- *Coordinates Pre- and Postmeeting Events.* The facilitator handles all arrangements to support productive meetings.
- *Seeks Clarity on Issues.* The facilitator clarifies the thinking of the group, often by pushing and prodding.
- *Assists Recorder.* The facilitator regularly summarizes and clarifies to help the recorder.
- *Plans Warm-Up or Other Opening Activities.* The facilitator organizes appropriate activities to start each meeting.
- *Plans Concluding Activities.* The facilitator organizes appropriate activities to end each meeting, summarizing accomplishments, identifying agreements, and listing next steps. Occasionally, the facilitator will lead a meeting or team appraisal process.

When to Use a Facilitator. A facilitator increases the likelihood that group members will accomplish the goals they set by keeping the group on task, focusing members' energy, making sure everyone has an opportunity to participate, and protecting group members from verbal affronts. The group's chair sometimes acts as facilitator, but some chairs are more like figureheads and acknowledge that they were not selected or elected for their meeting facilitation skills. Use a facilitator if the group is larger than just a few members, if the agenda requires much discussion or decision making, and if the group's dynamics are such that the group would benefit from a neutral manager.

When an issue generates a lot of emotion, especially when an internal facilitator might be considered to have a viewpoint, hiring an outsider can be especially useful. For example, as an outside facilitator, I once worked with an elementary school in which a particular group of parents wanted the school district to remove their principal. As facilitator, I was able to remind the parents that it was not their role or responsibility to hire or fire staff members. However, I was able to help the group identify the underlying issues in order for the district to begin to address the concerns of the parents. I interviewed individuals in advance of the meeting about their concerns with the leadership, and then when the group met, I was better able to draw out the issues when I felt the people weren't being completely honest or forthcoming in their responses. With so many people in the room feeling passionate about their views, the district leaders found it useful to have someone with an outside perspective leading that group's discussion. The parents felt they had been heard, and the district staff collected critical information allowing them to build an action plan to move forward. Many of the issues could be resolved and clarified.

The facilitator's job is to stay focused on the agenda and the group's desired outcomes. For example, when a group member starts a side conversation such as "Oh, that reminds me . . ." the facilitator's job is to honor the idea but find a way to guide the group back to the discussion. Some ideas include noting the idea on a chart called the "parking lot" or allowing members to write these thoughts down on index cards to be considered for a future agenda. We will discuss how to keep the group moving in Chapter 3, but the facilitator must be responsible for keeping the group moving toward its goal. A facilitator does not need to know anything about the subject matter the group is discussing, because the facilitator's role is to focus on the process. The facilitator's work is on the process, not the content.

The Timekeeper

The Role. The timekeeper is responsible for keeping the group focused on the task at hand by attending to the critical issue of time. The timekeeper monitors how long the group is taking to accomplish a task and calls the group's attention to the time remaining of the allotted time for a particular task, to help ensure the group will accomplish its desired outcomes. The timekeeper also keeps a record of the amount of time actually spent on an item and shares that record with the agenda planner. Using a timekeeper is an unemotional way to remind group members of the limitations of time they set for the meeting.

Qualities. The timekeeper must be able to attend to the meeting while also focusing attention on the amount of time being used on a topic. The timekeeper must also be able to tactfully work with the group to resolve time issues when discussions exceed their allotted time.

I was once part of a group in which the woman who was keeping time became more of a hindrance than a help. She gave out a time reading every 2 minutes: "You have 28 minutes left. . . . You have 26 minutes left. . . . You have 24 minutes remaining. . . ." That may be a slight exaggeration, but her habit of constant warnings was a distraction. She did not help the group. The timekeeper's job is to help the group.

How To. Participants may share responsibility for this role. The facilitator should not also serve as timekeeper since it is very difficult to track time when leading a discussion.

The group may wish to invest in a small digital timepiece with a stopwatch function. The timepiece should have a quiet alarm that, with minimal interruption, alerts the group or timekeeper that time is running short. It is the timekeeper's responsibility to work with group members to determine the details: whether they want a 15-minute warning or a 5-minute warning or whether they want to hear the alarm or have the timekeeper indicate in some way that the alarm has sounded, such as showing cards with the number of minutes left. Once the timekeeper knows the people in the group or group members get to know one another's preferred method, the task becomes easier.

When the timekeeper indicates that the available time is close to ending, the person responsible for the agenda item and the facilitator should have a sense of how close the group is to finishing the item. At that time, the timekeeper asks the group to choose among several options. The group may:

- finish the discussion and take the necessary action within the remaining minutes;
- request a time extension to finish the discussion;
- send the topic to a work team for further study; or
- table the discussion and put the topic on the agenda for the next meeting.

The person responsible for that agenda item or the facilitator should do the work of closing the matter. This is not the timekeeper's responsibility.

If the group decides to finish the discussion, members must agree to the consequences of that choice: The time allowed to discuss another topic may have to be shortened; another topic on the agenda may have to be tabled until the next meeting; or time for the meeting may have to be extended.

The timekeeper sometimes records the actual time spent in the meeting on each topic to help make necessary adjustments to the group's future agendas. Comparing the actual time to the planned time provides data for the agenda-builder planning. This comparison can also be used to inform the group about its meeting effectiveness.

Resources. A review of the description in this section and timekeeper's reflections will provide enough guidance to perform the role of timekeeper.

When to Use a Timekeeper. As a group works together, members will begin to understand the implications of not maintaining the schedule. Using a timekeeper will enable the group to become more efficient and effective.

One board I work with meets only a few times a year. Since members see each other infrequently, the group always begins with a time for each to share a personal update. It is a nice way to reconnect and to begin the transition to work in the meeting. Without a time-keeper, some members would likely give a much more detailed account of their lives, and the introduction to the meeting would end up taking as much time as the meeting itself.

The Recorder or Minutes Taker

The Role. Although the facilitator or other team members may take personal notes to help remember significant issues or actions, the designated recorder or minutes taker is responsible for maintaining the formal, public record of the meeting. The recorder supports the facilitator and the group by summarizing key ideas discussed, actions taken, and assignments made and then organizing data as they are reported. A recorder or minutes taker is often responsible for distributing the minutes to group members and designated others. This role is a good one to rotate because it requires a purposeful kind of attention and focus. A rotation schedule that occurs after several meetings, so the recorder gains experience, is usually more effective than making a change at each meeting.

Individuals will often say, "I'm not good at taking minutes." They want to pass the role and responsibility to someone else. So the person who is good at taking minutes ends up doing it over and over. The only way to get "good at taking minutes" is, in fact, to practice taking minutes. Like so many things, taking good minutes is a learned skill.

Qualities. The recorder should be someone with the ability to summarize major ideas without identifying every detail or every speaker by name. He or she must condense the main points of the group's discussion clearly and accurately into a simple format, articulating the group's agreements and recording action items. The recorder should be able to briefly describe objectives, accomplishments, decisions, and assignments. This person should have the resources to be able to produce and distribute the minutes to those designated to receive them.

Tip: The best way to become a skilled recorder is to do the job—practice!

How To. Minutes serve an important communication function, summarizing the key ideas the group discussed, actions the group took, and assignments made. The recorder makes notes throughout the meeting. Minutes always include *who* has agreed to do *what* by *when.*

After the meeting, the recorder uses the notes to briefly summarize the group's key findings. The length of the minutes depends on the detail those who attended want or need and whether summary reports, handouts, and so on are to be included. Different groups may require different amounts of information, depending on the individuals in the group or the group's responsibility for communicating with others.

The recorder must be disciplined and learn to synthesize, to identify key points, and always to include a decision so the group is clear about what occurred. When I first began, I wrote minutes that were five pages long: "Kathi said...." "Gina Marie said...." "Gary said...." Now, I just summarize key ideas. I note the topic, up to five or so key points that were raised, and any decision that was made. I just don't take down as much detail. People like it better because they don't like seeing themselves recorded by name as having said something, particularly if the topic was controversial. If people believe their names will be listed in the minutes, they may not say what is on their minds.

Resources. Handout 2.7: Minutes Format.

When to Use a Recorder. The group needs a recorder to prepare minutes if those attending the meeting want a reminder of what happened or a written record, or if people who did not attend the meeting need to know what happened. Groups that have long periods of time between meetings need a written record of the last meeting. The group might also want a summary of decisions and assignments.

> **Tip:** When the group has a low level of trust in the process or the meeting has dealt with detailed and complex issues, it can be helpful to use an LCD projector to display the recorded minutes at the subsequent meeting. Some groups might even choose to have an audio recording of the meeting as a backup.

The Scribe

The Role. Scribing is challenging and important work. A scribe allows important data/information to be displayed during the sessions and preserved. The scribe records ideas and information to use during a meeting to facilitate the group's discussion and focus the work. The scribe's job is to create a visual record of a meeting.

Qualities. A scribe must have good listening skills and be able to capture the essence of what participants say. Effective scribes spell well and write legibly. Scribes must be able to identify what has already been recorded and to accurately incorporate similar ideas from different participants. Equally important is the ability to synthesize information to capture thoughts without inserting one's own perspective. An ability to remain neutral and simply record the ideas is essential. Serving as the scribe can function as a way to involve individuals who might appear to be disengaged.

HANDOUT 2.7: MINUTES FORMAT

Group:

Date:

Time:

Participants:

Location:

TOPIC 1:

Discussion summary:

Decisions/assignments:

TOPIC 2:

Discussion summary:

Decisions/assignments:

General comments:

TOPICS FOR NEXT MEETING:

Next meeting date:

Time:

Location:

How To. The scribe creates the visual record without interjecting or usurping the role of the facilitator. An effective scribe must be careful not to take over for the facilitator, but to wait for the facilitator to provide clarification, if needed, before recording the ideas.

Before the meeting, the scribe and the facilitator need to work out a way to signal each other when either wants more information, when to quote the speaker exactly, and when to consolidate comments. In established and highly effective groups, skilled scribes may routinely interject, clarify, or paraphrase with the group's permission.

Skilled scribes in a group may want to rotate their roles even during a meeting so that each of them will have the opportunity in the same meeting to participate without having to scribe as well as participate.

Guidelines for the Scribe

- Write what people say. Do not change their words without their permission.
- Ask participants to summarize long ideas.
- Write clearly with black, brown, blue, or purple markers. (Some people have difficulty distinguishing reds and greens from a distance. Use lighter colors to underline, accent, or highlight.)
- When one sheet is filled, hang all of the working charts on the walls of the meeting room so that all ideas are visible to all participants.
- Make it clear to the group when you are contributing your own thoughts, ideas, and opinions.
- If the ideas are flowing too fast to record them all, ask for a second recorder to help move the group along and record all of the ideas that are being generated.

The scribe makes sure that the necessary supplies are ready before the beginning the meeting. These may include large sheets of paper on a pad or paper by the roll, an easel or wall areas for hanging the chart paper, masking tape or drafting tape to harmlessly post paper on the walls, pushpins if the paper will be affixed to a tackboard or fiberboard walls, or markers that don't "bleed" through the flip chart paper or smell too strong. During the meeting, the scribe records what people say without changing their words. If the idea is long, ask the group member to summarize it. Do not change a participant's words without his or her permission. Call attention to ideas that may need to be clarified so that everyone in the group understands what the speaker means. If a group member repeats an idea, ask how the thought is different from a previous one.

Make it clear to the group when you are contributing your own thoughts, ideas, and opinions. Create a symbol, insert your initials, or use a different-colored marker.

Write clearly with black, brown, blue, or purple markers. Some people have difficulty distinguishing reds and greens from a distance. Use lighter colors such as yellow, orange, or pink to underline, accent, or highlight.

When one sheet is filled, hang all the working charts on the meeting room walls so that ideas are visible to all participants. As you hang them, pay attention to how they are grouped. Because position helps to create meaning, the group may find it more useful to hang charts in the order they were created or to group them as they relate to topics discussed.

If the ideas are flowing too fast to record them all, ask for a second recorder to help move the group along and to capture all of the ideas being generated. Scribes can always request someone else to take their turn as scribe when they are uncomfortable with the role, want to participate, or are just getting tired.

> **Tip:** During a brainstorming session, a group may need several scribes to be able to keep up with the flow of ideas.

Occasionally, participants will make comments or suggestions not related to the topic. Establish a "parking lot" for these values, ideas, and points so that they are not lost. Remember that only the speaker can place an idea on the "parking lot." At the conclusion of the meeting, sort out which ideas might be dealt with immediately and which ones should be kept for further discussion.

Provide the written record to the facilitator or minutes taker to use when preparing minutes or reports. The notes that the scribe takes can also serve as a visual record and may be shared with others in accordance with the group's ground rules.

When to Use a Scribe. Use a scribe if the group will need a common set of data or information base for future reference. The scribe keeps a summary of the proceedings in front of the group and frees participants from taking notes. Using a scribe offers group members immediate feedback that their ideas, comments, and proposals have been heard and recorded. Participants are aware that all ideas are being considered. The visual record also provides a focus of attention during the meeting and can help the group gain a sense of accomplishment at the end as data are recorded and decisions are made. Not every meeting needs a scribe, but it is important to be prepared for times when such assistance is needed.

I worked with a board of education that was trying to set annual goals in a one-day session. We used a force field analysis tool (see Chapter 5, Handout 5.1: Force Field Analysis) to identify all the things board members thought they were doing well and issues they were facing. The trick was to get all those things down. We covered three walls with chart paper.

When all their thoughts were up on the paper, the group was able to "see" the challenges that were keeping them from achieving their goals. The groups used a prioritizing strategy (see strategies for

Figure 2.1   Sample Visual Record

Hamilton Park Pacesetter

Leadership Team Meeting, May 5, 2004

Facilitator: Liz Rowland
Recorder: Margaret Fair
Parent Rep: Mike Lanham

Warm-Up

Spend three to five minutes with someone you don't know well and find three things you share in common.

Research Update

Meg Quigley summarized research on the use of formative assessments. She shared the new common assessments developed by each grade-level team. Materials shared.

Integrated Curriculum

- Review implementation plans.
- Pam Bloom will present June 1–3 staff development program on using data from the common assessments.
- Tom Frank shared plans regarding the curriculum-mapping work in summer.

New Business

Sixth-grade teacher Sue Quinn presented an idea and requested feedback regarding a proposed fifth/sixth-grade "looping" design for 2004/2005.

Key Elements

- Students stay with fifth-grade teacher for either math/science or social studies/language arts block.
- Teachers of sixth grade will team with fifth-grade teachers.
- Students will stay in same group.
- Sixth graders will have opportunity to attend six-week special interest mini-courses.

Feedback/Comments

- How do we know this is best for students?
- Will there be a homeroom teacher?
- Who will teach Friday school?
- What about "Reach Students" who already miss Thursday?

Next Steps

- Teachers asked all members to submit questions/concerns.

Other Items

- Next Meeting: May 28, 2005

Facilitator: _____
Recorder: _____
Parent Rep: _____

narrowing choices in Chapter 4) to select five key issues to work on over a year. They could then move on to writing improvement goals. It was a simple process and got the work done in one day, and the scribe's recording was an essential element.

In another case, a district was completing a curriculum-mapping activity. Teachers covered the walls of the gym with the grade levels responsible for initiating, developing, and mastering each of the standards. When the group stepped back, they saw a clear problem: The teachers in the first three grades were responsible for initiating and developing some standards, but only the fourth-grade teachers had a requirement for mastery. The work of the scribe was drawing a great picture that accurately told the story. The visuals informed the group and its decision.

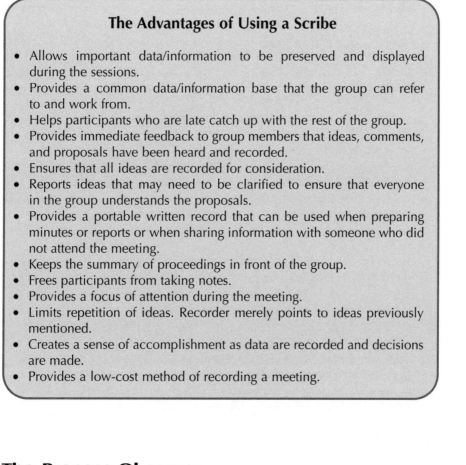

The Advantages of Using a Scribe

- Allows important data/information to be preserved and displayed during the sessions.
- Provides a common data/information base that the group can refer to and work from.
- Helps participants who are late catch up with the rest of the group.
- Provides immediate feedback to group members that ideas, comments, and proposals have been heard and recorded.
- Ensures that all ideas are recorded for consideration.
- Reports ideas that may need to be clarified to ensure that everyone in the group understands the proposals.
- Provides a portable written record that can be used when preparing minutes or reports or when sharing information with someone who did not attend the meeting.
- Keeps the summary of proceedings in front of the group.
- Frees participants from taking notes.
- Provides a focus of attention during the meeting.
- Limits repetition of ideas. Recorder merely points to ideas previously mentioned.
- Creates a sense of accomplishment as data are recorded and decisions are made.
- Provides a low-cost method of recording a meeting.

The Process Observer

The Role. A process observer remains outside the group, collects descriptive information, and provides feedback about what has happened during the meeting within the group so the group can reflect on successes and growth areas. Observations might include who talks to whom, what kinds of responses are given, what strategies group members are using, how the group accomplishes its work, and other insights. A process observer may be a member of the group or an external observer who agrees to attend one or more meetings to provide feedback.

Qualities. This role requires an insightful observer with experience working with collaborative processes and teams. A process observer must be discreet. He or she must use good judgment to determine which observations should be presented to the group and which should be offered privately to individuals. A process observer must be willing to give difficult feedback.

How To. If the group is willing to accept this type of feedback, the facilitator should help the group decide whether members wish to take turns serving as internal process observers or if they will enlist the services of an outside person. The facilitator confirms schedules for the observations and the feedback sessions.

Possible Topics for the Process Observer:
Things to Look For

- *Prework.* Was there prework? Did members come prepared for the meeting? Did members have an opportunity to influence the agenda? Was there a prepared agenda? Did it include desired outcomes?
- *Participation.* Did all members participate? Did all have an opportunity to participate? Did anyone dominate? Did anyone interrupt others?
- *Leadership.* Did a leader emerge? Was a leader designated? Who shared leadership?
- *Roles.* Were roles assigned? Did members accept or share responsibility? Who initiated ideas? Who helped push the decisions?
- *Decision Making.* Did the group determine the decision-making style prior to the decision? What processes did the group use to come to a decision? Did everyone accept the decision? Did anyone lead the group to the decision? How did members influence the decision?
- *Communication.* What verbal behaviors were apparent for each member? Did members interrupt one another, bring other members in, and demonstrate active listening? What nonverbal behaviors were apparent? Did the nonverbal behaviors contribute to the work of the group, or did they block progress?
- *Sensitivity.* Were members sensitive to the needs and concerns of others in the group? What evidence did you see?
- *General.* How well did the group work together? Did the group achieve its desired outcomes?
- *Recommendations.* What could the group do to work more effectively or efficiently?

SOURCE: *Leadership Through Quality: Interactive Skills Manual.* (1986). Rochester, NY: Xerox Corporation.

Group members next should decide on areas for observation. The group may want the observer to collect data about communication styles or patterns, leadership, roles, decision-making processes, use of tools and strategies for solving problems, how the group uses agendas or minutes, or other matters of concern. Starting with a limited focus, choosing two to four areas for observation is often the most effective path, and the focus can be extended as the group learns to use the information and feels comfortable with more feedback.

The process observer collects all information related to the purposes identified by the group. In the meeting, the process observer should remain physically separate, sitting outside the group's work area but still close enough to hear the conversations and observe nonverbal interactions.

The process observer may use a process observation form to collect data during the meeting. He or she also may use audio or videotape equipment to assist in collecting information. A process observation form is available in Handout 2.8: Process Observation Form. The process observer may modify the tool to respond to areas of need identified by the team. Handout 2.9: Communication Skills Data Collection Form for the Process Observer is another form that can help the process observer assess the group's communication.

After the process observer attends a meeting, the group schedules a time for the process observer to share data. The group discusses the information and avoids contesting the process observer's accuracy. After discussing the observations, the group decides whether any changes in behaviors, interactions, or processes need to be made. How a group responds to the feedback is critical. Groups that are open and prepared to develop a plan to improve based upon the feedback have the most success using this role. If a group is not willing to engage in this reflective practice, using a process observer does not make sense and is probably inappropriate.

A process observer may want to collect confidential evaluations from each person and compare the group results with his or her observations.

The process observer may also share information with individuals on the team. When the process observer has observed and recorded information about communication styles and skills, it might be appropriate for the observer to give feedback directly to each participant. Suppose that the observer noticed that one group member repeatedly interrupted and completed sentences for others. While that data would not need to be shared in front of the entire group, sharing the observation with the individual would be useful personally and could help the group function more effectively in the long run.

Resources. Handout 2.8: Process Observation Form (may be modified to respond to areas of need the team identifies) and Handout 2.9: Communication Skills Data Collection Form for the Process Observer.

(Text continues on page 74)

HANDOUT 2.8: PROCESS OBSERVATION FORM

Focus Areas	Team Member Name	Observation

HANDOUT 2.9: COMMUNICATION SKILLS DATA COLLECTION FORM FOR THE PROCESS OBSERVER

Directions

The process observer will record the times each team member uses one of these communication behaviors. (Remember the process observer can modify this form to collect data on a variety of other group behaviors.)

Behavior/Names	Sam	Susan	Frank	Tricia	Johnnie	Liz	Peter
Initiating							
• Proposing ideas							
• Building on ideas of others							
Reacting							
• Supporting							
• Disagreeing							
• Confronting/attacking							
Clarifying							
• Summarizing/ paraphrasing							
• Checking for understanding							
• Seeking information							
• Giving information							
Group Behaviors							
• Inviting active participation							
• Shutting out (interrupting, side conversations, etc.)							
Listening Behaviors							
• Attending/following							
• Reflecting							
• Summarizing							
• Nonverbal clues							

SOURCE: Adapted from *Leadership Through Quality: Interactive Skills Manual*, Rochester, NY: Xerox Corporation, 1986.

When to Use a Process Observer. A process observer can help a group improve its performance by providing feedback on how it is functioning. The facilitator may open a discussion with the group about the need to occasionally review the team's processes and behaviors. The facilitator and the team may discuss the benefits of this type of reflective practice.

A process observer is helpful when a group is struggling and is serious about improving. Observation can be particularly useful when the group does not understand why members are not reaching their desired objectives. One middle school learning team, for example, was committed to improving student achievement in language arts and met regularly to plan how to accomplish the goal. After many meetings, members hadn't noticed any real improvement in student learning. The process observer gathered evaluations, in which the members rated their communication as being highly effective. When the process observer attended the meeting, however, she heard conversations that mainly focused on student management. This discrepancy between the members' actions and the group's stated goal brought about a discussion that eventually resulted in the group getting back on track and focusing on learning issues that led to improved student performance.

I was once called in to observe a group that had gotten off track. It soon became obvious that two of the group members were having a serious disagreement that was hindering the team's work. When one would speak, the other would almost immediately cup his chin in his hand. When the other would speak, the first would get up to go to the restroom. While they never addressed each other directly, their behavior was so negative and exclusionary that it was obvious to nearly everyone else in the room. The other group members, however, felt it was not their place to address it. Bringing in a process observer relieved them of that responsibility. The trick for me as observer was determining the best way to make these two aware of their own patterns.

The process observer decides what feedback to give publicly and what needs to be private. I was once part of a group in which the process observer offered me private feedback after the meeting, letting me know he had observed that I interrupted others during the meeting. That was valuable feedback that nobody else had been tough enough to give to me. That experience made me more conscious of my own personal behaviors. That is not how I saw myself or how I wanted others to see me. That is when I became sold on the technique.

The Agenda Builder

The Role. Preparing the agenda is a powerful position and tremendous responsibility. It takes thoughtful attention to determine how the group will spend its time. This person or small group collects ideas or possible topics; determines what to address at the meeting; sets the time allotted for each topic; decides the category of the item, a discussion item or an action item; and determines the person who will be responsible. The agenda builder then prioritizes and produces the formal agenda and also distributes the agenda to each group member prior to the meeting according to the group's ground rules.

Qualities. Agenda builders need to have team members' trust. They must not let their own biases influence the priorities and must be perceived as fair. A good agenda builder is highly organized, detail oriented, and respects the process. They understand the power is in the agenda.

How To. When the team has clearly stated its purpose and nonpurpose, setting the agenda is much simpler. The agenda builder can then judge whether to place an item on the agenda by the item's congruence to the group's stated purpose. The agenda builder creates an agenda from items submitted for consideration by team members or others (parents, faculty, students, etc.) and from items identified during the last meeting.

Sometimes people submit ideas to the team that are not central to the group's mission. For example, a teacher may want someone to address how technology is distributed in the school and may submit the item to the school improvement team because that group is perceived as more powerful than the technology committee, where the issue would be more appropriately placed. The agenda builder for the school improvement team must keep the agenda aligned with that group's purpose to ensure a productive use of their limited time.

While an individual might take this task, a subgroup is often more effective, especially when conflicting priorities exist and decisions have to be made about the limited time that most groups have.

Distributing the agenda is also the responsibility of agenda builders. Teams can decide how far in advance they want to receive the agenda. There is considerable range in the amount of time before meeting members want their agendas. For some groups, 24 to 72 hours before the meeting is enough time to prepare. For others, depending on the length of the agenda and the amount of preparation needed, a week or more can be the norm. Members responsible for presenting or having responsibility for an item on the agenda should be given as much advance notice as possible so that they can adequately prepare.

At the end of each meeting, the agenda builder assesses the progress made toward achieving the stated desired outcomes. After each meeting, the agenda builder evaluates how well the agenda worked and uses that evaluation to influence the next agenda. The agenda builder also examines the timekeeper's time records to improve the accuracy of the estimated of times.

Resources. Review Chapter 1, "Building an Agenda"; Handout 1.4: Purpose/Nonpurpose Agenda; Handout 1.5: Contemporary Agenda Format; and Handout 1.6: Boxed-Agenda Format.

When to Use an Agenda Builder. Some groups may have reasons for building an agenda at the start of the meeting, such as a quickly assembled group during a time of change, but a more thoughtful, efficient process always involves a preset agenda. All groups need an agenda builder.

When a group includes different constituencies, one trick for successfully building the agenda is to be sure more than one person is involved. For example, one group I know includes the teachers' association representatives, principals, parents, and members of the board of education and the district leadership team. If the superintendent took responsibility for the agenda by himself, he could meet with resistance from the president of the education association, who might believe the superintendent was not representing members' interests. Instead, this group uses a subcommittee, in which one member from each group helps determine the items on the agenda. This group recognizes that power rests in the agenda. It is where priorities are set. In this group, the power is shared.

BUILD A KNOWLEDGE BASE

Teachers and others in a working group may need to develop greater content knowledge that is related to the group's goals. Committing to continuous learning will ensure decisions are made according to the best and most recent information, research, and knowledge of best practices.

One process for working together to improve members' knowledge base is a study group. Carlene Murphy and Mike Murphy (2004) provide a detailed account of forming a study group "where professional development activities converge and classroom implementation for the benefit of students is the focus" (p. 220). The processes that are used in student learning study groups can be applied to any groups in which a new knowledge base is needed to make informed decisions and achieve group goals. One feature of study groups is that members meet regularly for facilitated discussion of assigned readings or other sources of information.

One concern with this process is that some members may initially have difficulty committing to ongoing study outside the meeting times. The group needs to discuss its responsibility to "walk the talk"; if teachers expect students to improve through continuous learning, their own commitment to continuous learning is a powerful model.

If the group agrees to deeper study, members first must select the topic to be studied. The chairperson can lead the group in brainstorming a list of ideas. Individual members can volunteer or be assigned to identify sources of articles, books, videos, or people who could advise the group. Several good sources of material are the *Journal of Staff Development, Educational Leadership,* and *Phi Delta Kappan.* In addition, the Web site for the NSDC, http://www.nsdc .org, has a searchable library and a database of topics for members.

Searches through periodicals can also lead to a variety of references and other useful materials.

The facilitator, chairperson, or subgroup may select articles and make reading assignments for the group. Handout 2.10: Continuous Learning Log can help keep track of assignments during this process. Each participant then completes a study guide prior to the meeting based on the resource. (See Handout 2.11: Study Guide.)

During each meeting, group members spend 10 to 30 minutes discussing articles, books, and other resources related to the work. The group discusses key ideas and how those ideas might be applied in their work. The group may use Handout 2.12: Template for Analyzing the Logic of an Article. (See also Handout 2.13: Jigsaw Reading and Handout 2.14: Magnetic Questions for additional tools.)

Setting ground rules, identifying which roles will best serve the group, and assigning those tasks go a long way toward creating a highly functional group. Spending the time on these initial matters smooths the path for doing the work. I cannot overstate how essential the early preparatory work is for building a group that is able to work together effectively. A group that gets off to a strong start has fewer challenges in subsequent meetings. Still, no matter how hard we try, some issues are bound to arise. Meeting is relatively easy. Running a meeting that is effective and efficient requires developed skills. Those skills, and some possible challenges, are covered in Chapter 3.

> **Tip:** Create resource files to hold articles or reference on the key issues or priorities your group is organized to address.

HANDOUT 2.10: CONTINUOUS LEARNING LOG

Meeting Date	Key Topic for Study	Discussion Leader	Recommended Reference	Summary of Results/Findings

HANDOUT 2.11: STUDY GUIDE

Title of Article: _____

Source: _____

Significant Ideas: _____

_____

_____

_____

_____

_____

_____

_____

Implications for Our Work: _____

_____

_____

_____

_____

_____

_____

_____

_____

_____

HANDOUT 2.12: TEMPLATE FOR ANALYZING THE LOGIC OF AN ARTICLE

The Guide to Critical Thinking Concepts and Tools

Title of Article:

Source:

- The main purpose of this article is . . .
  (State as accurately as possible the author's purpose for writing the article.)

- The key questions the author is addressing are . . .
  (Seek ideas about the key questions in the mind of the author when he or she wrote the article.)

- The most important information in this article is . . .
  (Figure out the facts, experiences, data the author is using to support his or her conclusions.)

- The main inferences/conclusions in this article are . . .
  (Identify the key conclusions the author comes to and presents in the article.)

- The key concept(s) we need to understand in this article is/are . . .
  (Figure out the most important ideas you would have to understand in order to understand the author's line of reasoning.)

- The main assumption(s) underlying the author's thinking is/are . . .
  (Figure out what the author is taking for granted that might be questioned.)

- If we take this line of reasoning seriously, the implications for us are . . .
  (What consequences are likely to follow if people take the author's line of reasoning seriously?)

- If we fail to take this line of reasoning seriously, the implications for us are . . .
  (What consequences are likely to follow if people ignore the author's line of reasoning?)

- The main points of view presented in this article are . . .
  (What is the author looking at, and how is he or she seeing it?)

Discussion

These ideas could influence our work:

1. _____

2. _____

3. _____

SOURCE: Adapted from *The Miniature Guide to Critical Thinking: Concepts and Tools,* by R. Paul and L. Elder, 2004, Dillon Beach, CA: Foundation for Critical Thinking, www.criticalthinking.org.

HANDOUT 2.13: JIGSAW READING

Comments to the Facilitator

A jigsaw provides a good way for staff members to learn new content and also provides an opportunity for staff members to teach each other what they have learned.

Preparation

Make sufficient copies of the articles for each participant.

Note: Although individuals will be reading only one article, the principal should provide copies of each article for all staff members. Encourage them to collect the material in a folder or notebook for future review.

Directions

1. Provide three to five articles or share a longer article that has been divided into five sections.

2. Divide the school staff into the same number of small groups, trying to have three to five persons in each group.

3. Have each member of the small groups silently read one article or one section of an article. (Estimated Time: 10 minutes.)

4. Create new small groups from the individuals who have read the same material. Allow them time to discuss what they have read. (Estimated Time: 20 minutes.)

5. Re-create the original small groups. Have each person teach the rest of the group about his or her reading. (Estimated Time: 20–30 minutes.)

6. Conclude with the question: What are the implications of this for our school?

(Continued)

Handout 2.13 (Continued)

ARTICLE: _____

Highlights:

_____
_____
_____
_____

Implications:

_____
_____
_____
_____

Application:

_____
_____
_____
_____

ARTICLE: _____

Highlights:

_____
_____
_____
_____

Implications:

_____
_____
_____
_____

Application:

_____
_____
_____
_____

ARTICLE: _____

Highlights:

_____
_____
_____
_____

Implications:

_____
_____
_____
_____

Application:

_____
_____
_____
_____

ARTICLE: _____

Highlights:

_____
_____
_____
_____

Implications:

_____
_____
_____
_____

Application:

_____
_____
_____
_____

SOURCE: Reprinted with permission from *Tools for Schools*, December 2001/January 2002.

HANDOUT 2.14: MAGNETIC QUESTIONS

Purpose

This enables readers to identify key issues and underlying assumptions before they read. This is best used by a large group that will be reading a lengthy article or book together or viewing a videotape.

Directions for the Facilitator

1. Before the group gathers, write several key questions related to the reading or video. The facilitator should strive for provocative, thought-provoking questions. Write the questions on poster paper and post around the room.

2. After introducing the topic, invite participants to read the questions and choose one that appeals to or angers them.

3. Invite participants to stand by their chosen question.

4. Invite these small voluntary groups to talk with each other about what they find intriguing or important about the question.

5. After participants have talked about the questions, invite each group to report out or invite participants to individually speak up about what they discussed.

6. Capture on poster paper the big ideas raised by this group discussion. These questions can be used to guide the group's discussion after the group has finished its reading or viewing activity.

SAVE THE LAST WORD FOR ME

This additional strategy works best for groups reading articles, but it could be adapted for a book club by breaking down the book into chapters.

1. Have an entire group read the same article silently. (Prereading can be done to save group time for discussion.)

2. If the group is large, break down the larger group into smaller groups of five to six participants for this discussion.

3. Invite one participant in each group to begin by selecting one idea that they most want to share with others. There should be no dialogue during this sharing. Time: 2 to 3 minutes.

4. In a round-robin fashion, the next person suggests another idea. Again, no dialogue during this sharing. Time: 2 to 3 minutes per person.

5. Continue this until every participant has had an opportunity to talk. Continue doing rounds of sharing until participants have exhausted their comments or your time has expired.

SOURCE: Reprinted with permission from *Tools for Schools*, December 2002/December 2003.

3

Running a Meeting

t has happened to all of us. We are in front of a group, and suddenly we freeze. Time stands still as we try to remember the pertinent point we were going to present.

Or we are trying to lead, but no one seems to be following. The group seems particularly tired or distracted today. There is just no energy in the room. Some people in the group won't even make eye contact with the others. The shuffle of papers is the only sound.

Then there are times of tension. Disagreement within a group may get out of hand, nearly causing shouting matches between two participants. One group member's feeling of being personally attacked can leave wounds that take years to heal, and the group dynamics may become incredibly strained.

On the other hand, we have all been at meetings where the energy was palpable, where group members' smiling faces and body language immediately signaled how excited they were about the work. These people were comfortable with each other, were pleased to be present, and knew what they were doing there. People moved with purpose. The sound in the room was a low hum of voices. The air was alive with energy, and group members didn't need to be called to attention. They worked in synchronicity and harmony with one another.

While the group's development as a unit plays a role in making the difference between the earlier scenarios and the last, the skills of the group leader or facilitator also make a significant difference. These skills are gained over time, with experience and study. However, several tactics can help even a first-timer begin and run a meeting smoothly.

Facilitation Resources

Resources for learning more about facilitation skills include the following:

- *Effective Group Facilitation in Education: How to Energize Meetings and Manage Difficult Groups,* by John F. Eller (Corwin Press, 2004).
- *How the Way We Talk Can Change the Way We Work: Seven Languages for Transformation,* by Robert Kegan and Lisa Laskow Lahey (Jossey-Bass, 2002).
- *Mining Group Gold: How to Cash in on the Collaborative Brain Power of a Group,* by Thomas A. Kayser (McGraw-Hill, 1995).
- *Building Team Power: How to Unleash the Collaborative Genius of Work Teams,* by Thomas A. Kayser (McGraw-Hill, 1994).
- *The Adaptive School: A Sourcebook for Developing Collaborative Groups* (Chapter 6), by Robert Garmston and Bruce Wellman (Christopher-Gordon, 1999).
- *The Handbook for Smart School Teams,* by Anne Conzemius and Jan O'Neill (National Educational Service, 2002).

USE INTRODUCTIONS AND WARM-UPS

A colleague of mine once told me about a new group that she was beginning to facilitate in which one particular member was always careful to find out in advance whether she planned to use any sort of warm-up activity. Then he would show up 15 minutes after the beginning of the meeting. He didn't want to play.

Some people truly believe warm-up activities are a waste of time. The facilitator must gauge the group's interest and openness to getting to know one another in a way that is different from what everyday routine provides and then design the warm-up in a way that will be accepted by the group.

Introductions and icebreakers are useful when the group is just forming and members may not know one another. Even if some members of the group have worked together, introductions are a helpful way to begin to build a sense of group community, and participants still may find out things about each other that they didn't know. Introductions or warm-ups are a tool to ease the group into its work. Intimidating faces are less intimidating when introductions have been made.

Introductions and warm-ups should be short, generally no more than 10 or 15 minutes. The group's reason for coming together is to attend to its goals, and too much time spent away from that focus will dilute participants' sense of purpose and commitment to the process.

In choosing activities, the facilitator should note the group's culture and decide how best to meet members' needs and still fulfill the purpose of the warm-up.

One way to be sure that a warm-up is received well is to relate it closely to the day's task. One of my favorite warm-ups is a simple slide with the word "Courage" at the top. I ask each table group to define courage and talk about a time when they needed courage. I invite them to tell a story about what they would do if they had courage. A few guiding questions get the conversation started. I relate the word to the group's work: "Talking about courage is a related task, since right now what school leaders need is courage."

The conversations are brilliant. I have heard groups discuss how to teach courage, how to help kids say yes and no, and how to confront people when they are violating our beliefs. This type of warm-up is not soft, and groups have more patience with it.

When a group will be together for a long time and members need to know each other very well, warm-ups that help members know more about each other's character, rather than facts, are more useful. Ask about the highlights of a vacation and why those events stand out, instead of asking where they spent their last vacation. This reveals more of the individual's character. Be personal in a way that is connected.

While warm-ups should be brief, facilitators sometimes need to make judgment calls about how well they are achieving their purpose. For example, a district's leadership team recently had a retreat to spend the day discussing diversity. The district had been experiencing the kind of demographic changes typical of many smaller and midsized districts, and the topic was going to be key to the system's future success. During the first day's warm-up, each person was asked to tell his or her own story about identity.

The prompt was this: "Talk about a time when you experienced bias." Each person had a different cultural experience to relate. A man with a small build talked about his experiences with bias against his size. An African American man told a story about how a clerk regularly put his change on the counter instead of handing it to him. A female administrator told about a time she felt uncomfortable when a group of men stopped talking every time she walked in the room. It was an amazing sharing experience. The exercise took far longer than scheduled because this group participated with a true spirit of sharing and intention. It was very personal.

In the days that followed, we continued to build on that understanding. Each day's warm-up added a new facet. One day, we read an article about ways to talk frankly about race. The guiding question for the warm-up was "How do we tell the truth about issues that are related to race?" On another day, the prompt was "I learned something about my identity, my race, and my culture when . . ." This experience carried forward in individual relationships and whole-group work.

One of my favorite resources is *Energizing Staff Development Using Film Clips: Memorable Movie Moments That Promote Reflection,*

Conversation, and Action, by Walter R. Olsen and William A. Sommers (2005). On the last day this group met, we watched a clip from the movie *Sister Act* in which Whoopi Goldberg works with a group of nuns in a choir lesson. One woman wasn't singing in harmony, and we began a discussion of how being part of a team is different from a solo act.

I have used the barn-raising scene from the movie *Witness* to talk about structure and teamwork, *Twelve Angry Men* to begin discussions about conflict, and scenes of whitewater rafting as a segue in a meeting preparing parents, students, and staff for change. Perhaps my favorite is the chocolate factory assembly line scene from the *I Love Lucy Show,* which accurately portrays the increasing intensity of the reality of life in schools today. Film clips are a fun and relaxing introduction to the task.

An effective warm-up brings the group together in a new way, triggers conversations that are meaningful and related to the work,

Tip: Break a large group into smaller groups when asking individuals to speak during a warm-up to save some time, or set a limit for each person to speak. Vary the membership of the small groups.

and adds an additional dimension to how individuals relate to each other as they move forward. If the facilitator has not accomplished this goal, it is generally because of choosing the wrong activity for that group's culture or a decision that had to be made about time.

Below are some ideas for introductions or group warm-ups. Other ideas can be found in an Internet search with key words such as *introductions, tools, trainers,* and *icebreakers.* Other excellent resources a series of titles by Edward E. Scannell and John W. Newstrom, including *Games Trainers Play* (1980) and *Even More Games Trainers Play* (1994).

What's in a Name?

Ask individuals to take turns sharing how their parents chose their names or how they named their children.

Why Am I Here?

Ask each member to tell the group what he or she expects to accomplish through the group and why he or she is participating.

I find this especially helpful in nearly all situations. I always want to know why people are attending and what they hope to accomplish by participating. It is important to know whether it was compulsory that they attend. Starting this way eases my mind and also helps the group members to get to know one another.

Paired Introductions

Pair members and ask them to prepare a statement for the group introducing the other person. Suggest that they make sure to include the partner's name, position, areas of expertise, areas of need, and anything else you want to add to the list, such as a favorite book, movie, vacation, or story about a child. Groups can be creative and make this fun and unique.

Index Cards

Invite group members to write down questions they have about the initiative or what motivated them to participate in the work. Collect the questions and determine ways to respond. You might have other key individuals respond to some of the questions; you might address the questions in subsequent meetings; or you could reply in writing.

Two Truths and a Lie

If the group is larger, break it into small groups of five or six. Ask participants in the small group to introduce themselves by telling the others two things that are true and one lie. Others in the group then guess which descriptor is the lie. For example, I use as my Two Truths and a Lie that "I have a 27 handicap in golf, I used to work for Mr. Rogers, and I played the Mother Superior in a local production of *The Sound of Music*." One of those statements is a lie, and two are true. It will be up to you to guess which one of those statements is the lie. People generally share information that might not be known and might be fun for others in the group.

Wallets

Another warm-up that contributes to making a personal connection is "Wallets." Participants are invited to open their wallets and choose three things that will tell the group something important about them. Each person shares the three items with the group.

Warm-ups can continue to be used as the group progresses in its work. We can always discover new things about one another. Be sensitive to your group's willingness to participate in this kind of personal disclosure.

ORGANIZE SMALL GROUPS

When the working group is large, more than 10 or so individuals, some work is best done by breaking into smaller groups. Smaller groups are more useful when the work requires deep discussion among team members, when it makes sense to divide tasks, and often when you need to refocus the group's energy. Some members find it more comfortable to actively participate in the meeting when they are in smaller groups.

A superintendent once planned a gathering to get input about the district's future from members of the staff and the community at large. He wanted to know people's feelings about restructuring the schools' grade levels and about plans to address overcrowding in some areas. Anticipating the response, he set the meeting in the high school auditorium. The turnout exceeded his expectations. More than 800 showed up. Fortunately, seats were already set at smaller round tables, so groups were limited to eight as the work began.

In that example, it was easier to organize the crowd into smaller working groups simply through the room setup. In most meetings, breaking the large group into smaller teams may require the group leader to decide on a method for doing so.

While it is easy to use strategies such as asking people to turn to their neighbors to talk or to organize into small groups with those around them, there are times when the facilitator wants participants to have conversations with others in the room. Some useful strategies for arranging people into smaller groups are described as follows.

Lineup

This activity requires no advanced preparation.

There are many fun ways to have a group lineup. One way is to have everyone line up according to his or her birthday (month and date) without speaking. Once the line is in order, count out the number of people you need in each group. Invite people to line up by the model and make of their car or the number of years they have worked in a school or school district. Be creative and have fun with your line-up strategies.

Figure It Out

This activity requires bringing labels and some preparation in advance.

Determine the number of groups you need, and identify a category for each group. Categories might include presidents, sports figures, cartoon characters, and so on. Think of people in each category and write their names on labels. When the group meets, place a label on each group member's back and have each ask other group members three yes-or-no questions to help try to guess the person whose name is on the label. After members figure out their labels, they will easily be able to find their groups.

Marbles

This activity requires bringing marbles.

Have everyone choose a marble when entering the meeting. Use the colors to organize small groups.

Partners

This activity requires index cards and some preparation in advance.

Identify related pairs prior to the meeting, such as ham and eggs, king and queen, sun and moon, or peanut butter and jelly. Write each part of the pair on separate index cards. Hand each person a card as he or she enters the meeting. Ask group members to find their partners while they get their coffee or share a snack before the meeting starts. Once the pairs are identified, give each pair an assignment at the beginning of the meeting.

Puzzle

This activity requires bringing jigsaw puzzles.

Distribute separate puzzle pieces to each person entering the meeting, and have individuals assemble the pieces to find their group.

Royalty

This activity requires bringing playing cards and some preparation in advance.

Decide how many groups are needed, and separate cards by suit or by type, such as clubs, hearts, kings, queens, jacks, 10s, and so on. Give each person entering the meeting a playing card. Group members then find their "matching set" at the appropriate time.

Learning Buddies

This activity requires bringing a simple form for people to sign.

Decide how many activities require a partner. Prepare a form with lines for the number of "learning buddies." Ask the participants to make "learning buddy appointments" with others. Remind participants that when they make an appointment, they should write their buddy's name on the same line their buddy writes their name on.

Four Corners (or X Spots)

This activity may require some preplanning. It can also be done in the moment depending on the characteristics of the "corners."

Share a list of quotes about a topic related to the work of the team. Ask participants to choose from the topics and meet with others in their "corners" or "spots" in the room. They can talk briefly about why they chose the quotes and then begin the small-group assignment. Again, be creative about how to break the group into their corner groups.

A little imagination can lead to many more ideas for separating individuals into smaller groups. Many teachers have their own ways of doing so after years spent in the classroom. Ask group members for their ideas. More creative solutions exist than there are pages to list them.

BREAK UP THE TIME WITH ENERGIZERS

Energizer activities improve the meeting's quality and productivity. These activities can lower group members' anxiety levels, increase the group's energy, help direct individuals' thoughts along a different track, develop a comfort level among group members, and focus attention on specific themes related to agenda items.

Discuss with the group the purpose of using energizers and warm-ups. Ask the group to indicate where in the agenda members would like to use energizers and when they might find them distracting. Group members also can share responsibility for selecting and facilitating energizers. If they agree, ask them to offer strategies to determine who facilitates the energizer activities. For example, the group might decide to have meetings at different work sites and ask the host to be responsible for the energizers. Another option is for each member to take responsibility for energizers for a meeting selected in advance.

Energizers can be used to begin a meeting, after a break, when shifting to a new agenda item, to signal the need for a new type of thinking or behavior, or to reduce stress or revitalize group members after an intense discussion.

Energizers are helpful when the group has been sitting for more than 30 minutes. Simply getting up to stretch and move around creates more oxygen flow to the brain, which allows people to think more clearly. In *Teaching with the Brain in Mind*, Eric Jensen (1998) writes that, as oxygen is necessary for brain function, biology supports a link between movement and learning. The amount of oxygen transported to the brain is increased by enhanced blood flow, which can be increased through physical activity.

The person responsible or the facilitator should judge when to begin these activities. Energizers are helpful for breaking up long stretches of seat time, but remember that they may not be helpful if the group is feeling the pressure of a deadline.

An effective group leader monitors the group's pace and is sensitive to members' energy levels and focus. Pay attention to the nonverbal signs. The group will tell the story of what it needs. Members will begin to seem distracted, may be having side conversations, or may be so quiet they seem almost catatonic. If they are working in small groups, you may see some begin to stand up to take personal breaks.

Tip: Keep a list of energizers so you don't duplicate activities.

Energizers

- *Music.* Bring a CD player and play upbeat or dance music during the break.

• *Spinning Tops.* Have a contest spinning tops. Award a prize for the top that spins the longest.

• *Walk the Talk.* Make a processing assignment everyone can do with a partner while taking a walking break. Some processing assignments are as follows: Identify the three most important things you learned this morning; list the next three steps in this process; and reflect on the material we just covered and think of one way you will apply it to your work tomorrow.

> **Tip:** Make sure everyone in the group is physically able to participate in the specified activity.

• *Statues.* In this activity, participants relax their minds and bodies by acting like statues. The activity is generally more effective during the later stages of a program or session. It takes about 10 to 15 minutes, longer than the other energizers, and requires a space unobstructed by tables or chairs.

The leader asks the group members to stand and spread out so each has a space in which to move freely. The leader then tells participants that they will be doing an activity to help them relax their minds and bodies.

The leader explains that as he or she calls out the name or title of a statue from a list, all the participants simultaneously are to use their bodies to portray or interpret what the statue looks like. Group members hold their poses for five seconds and then relax their bodies as completely as possible. The leader waits 10 seconds and then gives the next title, and the process repeats.

The group leader then asks participants to portray a statue titled "Totally Relaxed." They hold their poses for one minute. To process the activity, the leader may have the group discuss how they felt before, during, and after the exercise and talk about the physical effects of work-related stress.

As an alternative, the leader could ask each group member to create his or her own statue and give it a name. Participants unveil their statues for the group one at a time. Another alternative is to have participants pair off and work with their partners to create, name, and act out statues with two figures, such as "principal and student," "learning," "athletes," or "the playground."

A suggested list of statues includes the following:

• Children at play
• Science teacher and high school student
• Paraprofessional and young child
• Cafeteria worker and seventh-grade student at lunch
• Runners at starting line
• Principal visiting a classroom
• Victorious athletes
• Teachers reflecting
• Custodian and high school student
• First-grade readers

- Music teacher and drummer
- School board member and parent
- Coach and track star

The most obvious element of energizers is also the most important: to get people up and moving. Sometimes movement can be built into the task at hand. The energizers that are also task oriented are my favorites, for example,

- Get three pieces of information related to the task at hand from three different people.
- Find somebody wearing the same color that you are wearing and ask that person how they have implemented one of the new strategies in their school.
- Look up and walk to the first person you lock eyes with. Talk with that person about . . .

Tip: Honor both introverts and extroverts by structuring activities that allow choice based on how different people are revitalized. Extroverts need other people for energy. Introverts often prefer to process individually.

- We're going to take a five-minute break. While you walk to the (restroom, coffee table), think of the three most important issues raised, and we'll discuss them after the break.
- Post chart paper around the room. Write a prompt at the top of each page and invite participants to wander around the room during a short break and begin to brainstorm ideas about each of the prompts.

To help group members choose energizers, give each member of the group directions for a variety of energizers, such as those discussed here and any others suggested by the group, to use at future meetings.

Resources for Energizers

Other sources for energizers include the following:

- *Energizers to Go! Super-Charge Your Training Sessions!* by Eric Jensen (Corwin Press, 2003).
- *Learning with the Body in Mind: The Scientific Basis for Energizers, Movement, Play, Games, and Physical Education,* by Eric Jensen (Corwin Press, 2000).
- *Getting Together: Icebreakers and Group Energizers,* by Lorraine L. Ukens (Pfeiffer, 1996).
- *201 Icebreakers: Group Mixers, Warm-Ups, Energizers, and Playful Activities,* by Edie West (McGraw-Hill, 1996).
- *The Big Book of Icebreakers: Quick, Fun Activities for Energizing Meetings and Workshops,* by Edie West (McGraw-Hill, 1999).
- *The Encyclopedia of Icebreakers: Structured Activities That Warm-Up, Motivate, Challenge, Acquaint, and Energize,* by Sue Forbes-Greene (Pfeiffer, 1982).

ASK QUESTIONS

Leaders and facilitators help groups achieve the results they desire by asking questions of members that clarify, confront, or prod their thinking.

One of the facilitator's most important responsibilities is using questions throughout the meeting to unlock the group's potential, uncover individuals' hidden agendas, ensure that all data and views are presented, and move a group closer to a consensus decision.

As Robert Garmston (2000) says,

> Conceptual levels are raised in an environment in which good questions are routinely asked. Research on teacher cognition reveals that teachers (as does everyone) make rational decisions based on simple mental models. As teachers reflect about their perceptions, assumptions, and data, their mental models become enriched and more detailed. Situations are understood in greater detail and from more perspectives. This increased information makes available more choices. More choices usually mean better choices. Teaching and learning are enhanced. (pp. 74–75)

Leaders or facilitators use different forms of questioning depending on what outcome they want. Although focused on student questioning, Blosser's (1997) ideas about types of questions apply equally well to adult groups. Knowing when and how to use questions is a skill that develops over time. Blosser says questions may be

- managerial, to keep operations moving (Is this item essential to the purpose? Can we have a moment of silence to think about our focus as a group? What steps do we need to take to accomplish this task?);
- rhetorical, to emphasize or reinforce a point (What I hear Sarah saying is . . . I think the group has reached a consensus about . . .);
- closed, to check participants' understanding of the issue (Jorge's idea is . . . Before we move on, does anyone want to add his or her thoughts? Does everyone agree that . . . ?); or
- open, to promote further thinking and discussion (What results do we want? How do we want to proceed . . . ?)

The leader or facilitator should pause for some time after asking a question or making the statement to allow time for group members to process their responses. After a group member or members have responded, pause again to give responders time to add to or modify their responses or to allow comments from others on what has been said. Silence is not only golden, it sometimes yields precious nuggets.

In addition, the questioner's word choice and tone of voice are very important. Questions should be tactful rather than confrontational. Use language that is neutral, does not suggest authority, and proffers choices to the listener. The questioner's tone of voice should be genuine and relaxed, reflecting a true desire to listen without judgment. Statements used to spur group members to think still should end on an up inflection, to diminish the speaker's perceived authority and give control to the group.

I often make a statement to evoke the group's reaction, to get members talking. I might say, "I question our plan for full inclusion," to prod the conversation along. By declaring a position, others can react. Dennis Sparks in *Leading for Results* (2005) reminds us that "questions are often an indirect and less efficient method of stating assumptions and intentions, making requests, and deepening understanding. In addition, questions that are knowingly or unknowingly intended to elicit a particular response often induce anxiety or defensiveness" (pp. 66–68). It is possible to generate more conversation without using as many questions but rather by making simple declarative statements stating opinions, assumptions, and ideas.

It is possible, as the facilitator, to follow up this open discussion with questions that generate action planning: "What steps do we need to take to make this work? What needs to be done before . . . is possible?"

One of many valuable lessons I learned from Dr. W. Patrick Dolan, of W. P. Dolan and Associates, is to arrive early and spend time listening prior to a group meeting if you are an outside facilitator. He taught me to listen for the underlying issues, to try to sense what might be going on, and to try to understand the system and culture at work within the group by talking informally with individual members. When he goes to work with a new group, he schedules briefing phone calls and then arrives early in the morning, walks around informally, and simply asks, "How's it going?" By pausing long enough, he receives honest responses. He is present in that moment. Once people believe he is not merely asking the courtesy question but is really listening, they tend to open up in their responses. Then he follows up by asking where the group is getting stuck. By listening for their stories, he is able to glean information they may not even know they are giving, putting pieces together with others' information to create a fuller picture of the tasks ahead. He listens for speakers' word choices, their inflection, where they hesitate, the topics they shy away from, and words or phrases that seem to repeat from individual to individual that may be code for underlying issues or practices within that school culture.

Facilitating open dialogue and informal conversations provides the facilitator or group leader with information for telling stories, base additional prompts and illuminates key issues for the group. Although learning how to listen deeply, identifying which questions to ask, and inviting open responses takes time, it is one of the essential skills of good facilitation.

MANAGE THE CHALLENGES

A variety of personalities and styles can emerge during meetings. Sometimes, individuals are positioning themselves during critical times.

Other times, it could be a matter of personality. It is said that in any group, 8% will be innovators, 17% will be leaders, 29% will be early adopters, 29% will be late adopters, and 17% will be resisters (Rogers & Rogers, 2003). Dealing with resisters or difficult people can be challenging. Sometimes, individual styles interfere with the group's effectiveness. Meeting effectiveness can be improved if the facili-tator or group leader and group members have tools to use when facing challenges.

I learned very early in my work as a facilitator that there will be many different ways to respond in every given situation. The dynamic of each group is unique. It helped when I learned that there is often a reason for why people are responding the way they do. In fact, when I can slow down my reaction time, I generally make a much better intervention. It helps to discuss the possible reasons someone might be responding in a certain way. For example, someone who is unusually quiet may be an introvert who is more likely to open up in smaller groups, or may have been put down at another meeting and so resists speaking to avoid that experience again. (See Handout 3.1: Plan Your Response to Difficult Participants.)

Here are several other challenging situations that facilitators face and how you might respond.

One basic tool for responding to unproductive behavior is *proximity*. In a group setting, the facilitator's physical proximity can be used as a calming and reassuring force when a group member is out-of-bounds. Standing nearby lets that person know he or she is being heard, and the facilitator may be able to redirect the conversation using body language, for example, making eye contact with the speaker and then shifting focus to another group member, a light touch on the person's shoulder, or changing position to face a different speaker.

> **Tip:** Don't get flustered. Remember, the behavior likely isn't directed at you. Stop and breathe. Ask yourself, "What could be triggering this person's behavior?"

Another key in challenging times is quite simple: Breathe. Allow a few seconds of silence. Collect yourself and breathe deeply. Oxygen is necessary for the brain to process thought. And silence can produce other unexpected results within the group.

Understanding is imperative. We should remind ourselves to approach every situation with kindness and the expectation that the other person is working from a position of good and that he or she also has the best possible end in mind. Even if that person is not approaching the matter in the same way we would, he or she may still have positive intentions.

I am often frustrated by participants who volunteer to do something and then don't deliver. If it happens once, I can be very patient. However, when it happens regularly, I find it difficult. So, I slow down and wonder, what would make this person volunteer when he or she clearly can't deliver on a promise? I can come up with a million good reasons: This person wants to be helpful, wants to be an active part of the group, and wants to serve—and yet may not have realistically looked at the schedule or just took on too much.

HANDOUT 3.1: PLAN YOUR RESPONSE TO DIFFICULT PARTICIPANTS

Q: Every meeting I run seems to have at least one person who causes a problem and prevents the rest of us from dealing with the issues at hand. In the end, all of the participants feel like the meetings have been a waste of their time instead of producing the results we need. What can I do?

A: Well, you're not alone. Anyone who's ever run a meeting has encountered difficult participants. Some passively resist becoming involved; others aggressively try to thwart your efforts to achieve something. No single response is appropriate for every participant.

Training magazine (July 1998) offered these tips for dealing with difficult participants at meetings. As you consider *Training* suggestions, keep in mind that it's best to deal with disruptive individuals in private and after meetings.

The Warm Body. This person doesn't participate. He just sits there, not even offering an affirming nod of the head. Try direct questions to draw him into the action.

The Side Conversationalist. This person always has distracting conversations with people sitting next to her. Ask her to stop.

The Interrupter. He constantly breaks in to forward his own agenda. Ask him to wait his turn.

The Competitor. She wants to win every point. Remind her that other solutions deserve to be explored.

The Joker. This person's constant jokes distract others. Tell him so outside of the meeting.

The Windbag. This spotlight hog eats time with war stories. Cut him off. Tell him others have things to say and time is limited.

The Factionist. To persuade others to agree with her, she tries to form coalitions to pressure the group to accept her ideas. Point out how destructive her behavior is. If she doesn't stop, don't invite her to future meetings.

The Sarcastic One. This person can't resist a snide remark. He belittles what others say. Tell him to keep such comments to himself.

The Objector. "It'll never work" is this person's mantra. No ideas suit her. Tell her to make her criticisms constructive.

SOURCE: Reprinted with permission from *Tools for Schools,* October/November 1998.

Another person's method may not be to my liking, but if I judge everyone according to the way that I would accomplish the task, I would be wrong. Assuming that group members have good intentions can help keep the facilitator from being unkind, short-tempered, or frustrated by the disruption to the group process.

> **Tip:** In some situations, the facilitator may take an unscheduled break to talk individually with someone whose behavior is affecting the group adversely.

Many years ago, I was attending a keynote address, and a person had forgotten to turn off his cellular phone. Of course, the phone rang in the middle of the presentation. The consultant at the event made an embarrassing situation worse by stopping the speech and publicly chastising the audience member. I never want to embarrass someone, particularly in front of the group. Most (and I hope all) people recognize that there is appropriate cell phone, personal digital assistant (PDA), and pager behavior. Use the moment to remind everyone to silence the tones, without attacking the culprit.

If a group member is persistently difficult, I generally approach the situation using increasingly strong interventions. I always begin with a private intervention. Pointing out observations about the individual's behavior in a one-on-one conversation may lead both the facilitator and the group member to a greater understanding of the cause of the individual's actions. The person may not have recognized his or her own behavior or may not have seen it as a disadvantage. It is important for the facilitator to approach these difficult conversations without judgment. Try to open a conversation to discover the underlying issue.

> **Tip:** Individuals often act out of frustration when they think they are not being heard. Simply making a visual record of their idea for all to see can reinforce that someone is listening.

Negative behavior that continues after an individual conversation may be changed by the second intervention, that is, by using peer pressure. Without identifying the offending individual, it might work to remind the group to talk about its ground rules. Try to get members to identify any rules being violated and talk about how to get back on track together.

Sometimes groups include a single-issue person who wants to make a point and persists despite any subtle redirection. In these cases, the third intervention might be made when the facilitator stops the person and, while reinforcing that the issue is an important one, reminds the speaker that this point is not a matter for this group or is directing the conversation off task. Singling out the person in front of others is not a common or preferred response. The last resort and the most dramatic intervention would be to ask the person not to serve on the committee.

Another common situation is side conversation. Again, a belief in positive intentions helps. Most of the time, side conversations are on task. Two people may be talking to clarify a point they didn't understand. If several groups are talking, the facilitator may want to have the group take a break, honoring members' positive intentions and respecting their need to clarify the issue. They may need some time to talk about the task to understand it better. It is also possible that group members may need some time away from the task to reenergize.

Tip: If many in the group are talking, break up into small groups to help group members process. Doing so honors members' needs.

Some group members will be especially verbose. These may be people who tend to think out loud, without much forethought. Sometimes they may be the less articulate, but most often they are extroverts who externally process information. In any group, time is limited, and allowing speakers to ramble is unproductive. One quick way to intervene is to ask the group to stop and take 10 minutes in smaller groups to come up with three points. In a small-group setting, peers can question and probe within a time limit to help the individual become clearer or move on.

Challenges in the Meeting

If you face one of these situations, here are some ideas about how to respond:

1. Comments are made that indicate a lack of understanding of an agenda item.
   - What is the purpose of this agenda item?
   - Why is this item essential?
   - What questions do we want to have answered about this agenda item?
   - What are we trying to accomplish?

2. Comments are straying from the agenda item under discussion.
   - What did we say we are trying to accomplish with this discussion?
   - Could we please return to the agenda item under discussion?
   - Could we place that idea on our parking lot and return to our stated outcome?

3. Issues or topics are being raised that are not on the agenda.
   - Could we please record this topic and add it to the next meeting agenda?
   - Does this group want to amend the agenda to include this item?
   - Do we want to reconsider our agreement to address only those items on the final agenda?

4. Agenda time allotments are not being followed.
   - We are past the allocated amount of time for this agenda item. Do we want to stop discussion, send the issue to a small group for further study, or place the item on the agenda for the next meeting?
   - If we want to continue discussion on this topic now, how do we want to adjust the remainder of the agenda?

5. Side conversations are taking place among group members.
   - What are the norms we established regarding attention during meetings?
   - Is anyone finding the side conversations distracting?
   - Do we need a break in order to process this information?

6. The group is restless, disinterested, distracted, and bored.
   - What are you thinking/feeling right now?
   - Do we want to alter the process we planned? Do we need more opportunities to move around?
   - Do we need a break?
   - Would someone else like to take a turn facilitating, recording, or timekeeping?
   - Why don't we all change seats or stand for a moment?

7. The discussion is circumventing the genuine underlying concern or point.
   - Is there something underlying this discussion that we aren't articulating?
   - What are you thinking that you aren't saying?
   - Why did you say what you just said?
   - What are the assumptions that are underlying the key issues here?

8. Group members are not expressing what they really think or want.
   - Are you saying everything essential to this point?
   - Would you say we are getting everyone's honest opinion?
   - What have you heard others saying about this issue?

9. Some individuals are not contributing to the meeting.
   - Will you please write your thoughts on an index card anonymously and turn the papers in on your way to the break?
   - Is there anything we need to do to ensure that everyone contributes?
   - Why are we not hearing from all the members of the group?
   - Shall we try a round robin to get every voice in the room before we go any further?

10. The group is being dominated by one or more people.
    - Can we please limit our individual remarks to two to three minutes on this topic?
    - Could we break into small groups of three to four people and reach consensus on . . . ?
    - Would you (the dominant individual) please serve as the recorder of the group memory?
    - If anyone has additional thoughts on this topic, would you please see me at the break?

11. The group is not thinking win-win.
    - Could we articulate one list that summarizes the desired results of all group members?
    - What are some solutions that will produce the desired results of all group members?
    - What are the critical attributes of a win-win solution for this situation?

(Continued)

(Continued)

Situations/Questions Relating to Process

1. Individuals are making speeches and preventing the group from taking action.
   - Do we want to put a time limit on this discussion?
   - By what time do we want a decision?
   - Can we save time by providing everyone who wants to comment with two to three minutes to speak?

2. An agreement on a decision cannot be reached.
   - Could you please pair up with someone who disagrees with your position? Now, take the position opposite your own and argue for it. Have the other person do the same. Does your position change or stay the same?
   - Could we have a small group consider this decision during the break and make a recommendation?
   - Could we have a subgroup consider this decision and have a recommendation ready by the next meeting?

3. The group is not adhering to agreed-upon roles.
   - Could you each take a minute to review the responsibilities of your own role?
   - How can we pay better attention to the roles we agreed to assume?
   - How can we help each other do this?

Situations/Questions Relating to Meeting Outcome

1. The group is failing to produce creative alternatives to current problems.
   - What are the results we desire?
   - How are the proposed solutions different from what we are currently doing?
   - Are the proposed solutions sufficiently different to produce the desired results?
   - What are some processes we can use to generate creative alternatives?

2. The group does not have enough information or expertise to analyze the problem and solve it.
   - What information is still required to analyze the problem and solve it?
   - What sources can we use to help us come up with ideas?
   - How can we obtain the information we require in the most timely way?
   - What skills are essential for solving this problem once the information is available? Can we brainstorm to help us problem solve?

3. The final decision maker(s) is(are) not present.
   - Who has the power to say "yes" to implement the decision?
   - Who has the power to say "no" to our decision?

- What is the best way, and who is the best person to talk with the decision maker?
- What are leveraging points to make in trying to sell the decision?

4. There is a decision under discussion that may produce extreme pressure on individuals or the group (for example, an unrealistic timeline, funding implications).
   - What are the steps required to accomplish this task?
   - How long will each step take?
   - Which individuals are responsible for each task?
   - What support do these people require?
   - What are the implications of the decision for the individual(s) responsible and the group?

The facilitator or leader may choose to spend some or all of a session on developing group members' own skills for dealing with difficulties.

In addition to facing challenging situations from individual group members, the facilitator or leader can sometimes face issues related to the group's work. The most common is when one group member offers an example and others follow with story after story, leading the group away from its purpose. The facilitator's job is to help the group stay focused. The facilitator may stop the conversation and ask the group for three good examples and, then, given those conditions, three strategies to address the issue.

> **Tip:** As the facilitator, approach a difficult situation with a group member from the perspective of "How can I best get around this moment without being mean?"

Groups can be quickly redirected using simple structures. Knowing where the group stands, often from information gleaned in earlier conversations, can aid the facilitator in doing the job. A good facilitator keeps his or her focus on the people and the task.

Storytelling is another tool that can redirect the group. With one group, for example, my colleague and I picked up on dissension between the staff and the school administrative team. Early conversations hinted at the issue more by what teachers would *not* talk about than what they did say. In facilitating their meeting later, I told the group a story about a group of teachers who had told me that their principal had brought a great idea to the faculty for a vote and they unanimously voted no. I asked them why, and they whispered that they did not like the principal and therefore could not support ideas

> **Tip:** Have the group agree on a friendly signal to remind individuals when they are exhibiting unproductive behavior. Groups have used foam balls, friendly verbal reminders, or the universal time-out sign.

that he brought to the group. What I learned from that group is that the message often gets lost with the wrong messenger. And the group

I told the story to learned that they needed to be more reflective, focusing on the idea, not just the messenger.

That group and others with whom I've shared the story heard the message. I tell the story in a way that doesn't target the current group's principal as the culprit for the challenge within the group. When groups hear the message from a personal story, however, they may open up the conversation about the reasons for their own resistance.

Some leaders and group facilitators may feel personally involved in group challenges. It is important that we keep the work apart from us as people. One thing I've learned is that most things I think are problems today become stories tomorrow. Only a few are really significant enough to remain real problems. I ask myself, "Is this going to be a problem next week?" Most of the challenges I face will not fit the criteria of a lasting problem.

Most problems are really inconveniences. Most are solvable. Through proximity, questioning, silences, or storytelling, good facilitators and strong leaders learn to redirect the group in challenging times, whether the issue is one of personalities or of process. The best way to develop the skills to meet these challenges is to add tools to one's repertoire.

Meeting these types of challenges is, well, challenging. At the end of a difficult meeting, it can be tempting to close quickly. However, an effective meeting requires a smooth ending.

CLOSE THE MEETING WELL

The close of the meeting mirrors some aspects of the introduction. Just as the facilitator lays out the expectations and agenda at the beginning, the facilitator needs to sum up and restate the work at the end. We want to complete the meeting as quickly as possible and be efficient, so group members can go on to other important tasks, but taking time at the end of business to carefully summarize is about as important as the time spent planning before the meeting.

The facilitator or group leader should end actions and other discussions 10 or 15 minutes before the scheduled meeting end, to allow for closing and debriefing. If the team has established sound ground rules and meeting procedures, team members will respect and come to value the time spent closing and debriefing the meeting. Use the following series of specific steps to bring the meeting to a successful close. (Handout 3.2: Closing a Meeting Successfully can be used as a form for notes for your specific needs.)

Review Unfinished Business

The facilitator begins the wrap-up by taking care of "leftovers." The facilitator reviews agenda items not completed or not discussed and reflects upon "parking lot" items. Discuss with the group whether to place these items on the agenda for the next meeting, whether

HANDOUT 3.2: CLOSING
A MEETING SUCCESSFULLY

☐ Take care of leftovers.

☐ Review action items. Review assignments.

☐ Highlight items for the next session.

☐ Debrief.

☐ Assess the work of the team periodically.

additional preparation or premeeting materials are needed to discuss or take action on these items at the next meeting, and who is responsible for each task related to the items.

Review Action Items

The facilitator reviews all decisions made during the action discussions. Reviewing decisions gives the group a sense of accomplishment and ensures that all members understand the agreements that were made.

Review Assignments

The facilitator reviews all assignments. This review of tasks that need to be accomplished helps a group to be more productive. It also helps team members to acknowledge the need to equally share the workload. It becomes apparent if one or two people are accepting all of the assignments or others are not participating in the completion of the work. This review helps groups become more accountable.

Highlight Items for the Next Session

The facilitator highlights all items that have been identified during the meeting that need to be addressed at the next meeting. Some groups also draft the next agenda and identify group roles for the next meeting.

Acknowledge the Group's Work

Acknowledging the team's work and celebrating accomplishments helps build group members' sense of satisfaction; positive emotional responses to one another and to the process, which is a valuable component of learning; and commitment to the group.

A group that meets infrequently, two or three times a year, generally makes time at every meeting for these acknowledgments. Other groups may decide for themselves how frequently to celebrate and how they want to do so.

Many different activities can help close on a positive note. In addition to those listed here, more activities can be found in several of the books on energizers and icebreakers listed in the "Extended Readings" section of this book. The following are some activities to use:

- *Pipe Cleaner.* Ask everyone to create a symbol with pipe cleaners of what they "take away" from the group.

- *Pat-on-the-Back.* Ask each member to compliment another group member's contribution.

- *Squishy Ball Rally.* One member of the group tosses a squishy ball to another, who must then make a comment about the group's work. The leader might ask that members finish an open-ended phrase: "This meeting was successful because . . ." or "Next time, let's not forget to . . ." Use a variety of sentence starters to draw the work of the team to a close.

- *Build a Puzzle.* Buy foam board and cut it into as many puzzle pieces as there are team members. Give one puzzle piece to each person and ask that person to draw a picture on that puzzle piece of the contribution he or she made to the group's work. When everyone is done drawing, ask them to put the puzzle together and tape the back, creating an artifact documenting everyone's efforts.

- *Secret Pals.* Assign each member a secret pal and ask the pal to give written feedback to the person whose name he or she drew. Give members time at the end of the meeting to write their notes. Collect the notes and hand them out anonymously.

Appraise the Meeting

On occasion, the facilitator needs to hold a session critique or meeting appraisal. Depending on how often the group meets, perhaps a couple times a year for a group that meets regularly, teams that want to improve their procedures or practices need to take time to reflect on their processes and identify areas for improvement.

Sometimes these appraisals can point out real group dysfunction. One school staff, full of really bright people, had ongoing difficulties accomplishing work in their leadership team meetings. Finally, the group did an appraisal of their work as a team. The first item on the assessment read, "I speak clearly and to the point." All members rated themselves at the top of the scale. The second item read, "Other members of this team speak clearly and to the point." They all rated every other person in the group at the bottom of the scale. All I had to do was to report the data and stand back. They could look at the results and see their foolishness. From there, the facilitator asked them for next steps; they set some ground rules and determined a process for making decisions and set up standing committees for work, and the impasse was broken.

In another case, with a board of directors, group members were asked to respond to the statement "We respect diverse opinions." Ten of the 12 members gave the group high marks. Two people, however, scored the board very low. Rather than looking only at the average, the facilitator looked more closely at the two low scores and saw immediately that both the individuals who rated that item as low were African American. She quietly asked the two if they would share their experiences with other board members, and they told stories of times when they felt others were not respectful or inclusive. Their insights led to a fierce conversation and a commitment to improve. The two promised to speak out more; the 10 gained a new perspective on their own actions; and all learned a powerful lesson. All they had to do was be willing to ask the question, "How are we doing?"

Those last few minutes of the meeting, combined with using the assessment, made every meeting afterward much more productive.

Groups can use the meeting appraisal guide sheets in this book (see Handout 3.3: Meeting Debriefing Surveys and Handout 3.4: Team Meetings) or adapt them to suit the group's purpose. The meeting appraisal formats are designed to address different types of issues during the critique. Groups may want to use more than one of these formats over the time that the team works together. The facilitator should lead a discussion of the purpose of the meeting appraisal process to ensure the group's willingness and commitment to listen to the information gathered and to respond to it with fairness and honesty, even when the data are difficult.

I have learned in working as a facilitator to be intentional, to plan, to modify as necessary, and to tell the stories when they need to be told. Knowing how to open and close the meeting; knowing when to question, when to make declarative statements, and when to stand back; and knowing when the group needs a break and when to offer an energizer are all matters of listening. If you listen carefully and closely and not just to what people say on the surface, not just to their words, the group will tell you what you need to know to successfully lead a meeting.

HANDOUT 3.3: MEETING DEBRIEFING SURVEYS

Comments to the Facilitator

These tools will assist various teams in assessing how well they attend to the basics of successful meetings. In order for this tool to be used effectively, team members must have agreed on a set of norms ahead of time. This tool would best be used after the team has met several times and can gauge the team's attention to its goals.

The team can add its own norms in order to adapt this tool for its unique needs.

Ensure anonymity for respondents by having team members fold their surveys and drop them into a box.

Calculate the results privately and share the total results with the entire group publicly during the next team meeting.

Lead a discussion about possible implications of the responses. *In what areas is there already substantial agreement that the team is performing well together? What areas does this team need to work on? What are some strategies for improvement in that area?*

What feels right for you?

_____

_____

_____

What is going well for the group?

_____

_____

_____

Where are we struggling?

_____

_____

_____

How do we want to improve?

_____

_____

_____

What do we want to remember for next time?

_____

_____

_____

(Continued)

Handout 3.3 (Continued)

Meeting Evaluation Form

How valuable was the meeting?

A waste of time   1   2   3   4   5   **Extremely valuable**

Comments: _____

_____

_____

_____

How effective was the facilitator?

Very ineffective   1   2   3   4   5   **Extremely effective**

Comments: _____

_____

_____

_____

How effective was the recorder?

Very ineffective   1   2   3   4   5   **Extremely effective**

Comments: _____

_____

_____

_____

How much were you able to contribute to the meeting?

I did not feel that my   **I felt that my idea/**
input was considered 1   2   3   4   5   **recommendations**
                                                  influenced the group

Comments: _____

_____

_____

_____

What suggestions do you have for improving the next meeting?

_____

_____

_____

_____

Thank you for your thoughtful responses to the debriefing process.

Meeting Appraisal Form

Modify the appraisal form to monitor the work and the focus of the group. Identify issues that need to be examined and prepare a scale to assess the issue.

1. We hold meetings only when we have a valuable agenda.
   ⇐ **Never   Infrequently   Sometimes   Regularly   Consistently** ⇒

2. The agenda is clear and directs the work of the group.
   ⇐ **Never   Infrequently   Sometimes   Regularly   Consistently** ⇒

3. Group members appear committed to the work.
   ⇐ **Never   Infrequently   Sometimes   Regularly   Consistently** ⇒

4. The group adheres to its ground rules.
   ⇐ **Never   Infrequently   Sometimes   Regularly   Consistently** ⇒

5. The group has the knowledge base to reach its decisions.
   ⇐ **Never   Infrequently   Sometimes   Regularly   Consistently** ⇒

6. Meeting energizers are timely and used appropriately.
   ⇐ **Never   Infrequently   Sometimes   Regularly   Consistently** ⇒

7. Minutes are clear and accurate.
   ⇐ **Never   Infrequently   Sometimes   Regularly   Consistently** ⇒

8. Attention is paid to completion of tasks as well as to relationships.
   ⇐ **Never   Infrequently   Sometimes   Regularly   Consistently** ⇒

9. Time limits are respected.
   ⇐ **Never   Infrequently   Sometimes   Regularly   Consistently** ⇒

10. Decisions are reached by consensus.
   ⇐ **Never   Infrequently   Sometimes   Regularly   Consistently** ⇒

11. The group uses alternative strategies to solve problems.
   ⇐ **Never   Infrequently   Sometimes   Regularly   Consistently** ⇒

12. Action plans and charge statements facilitate the effectiveness of the group.
   ⇐ **Never   Infrequently   Sometimes   Regularly   Consistently** ⇒

13. Contributions are recognized and valued.
   ⇐ **Never   Infrequently   Sometimes   Regularly   Consistently** ⇒

14. Commitments are honored by group members.
   ⇐ **Never   Infrequently   Sometimes   Regularly   Consistently** ⇒

(Continued)

Handout 3.3 (Continued)

Learning Team Survey

Remember, you may use part or all of this survey.

School _____

Subject/Grade Level _____

1. How many times have you met with your learning team?

   1–3 _____   4–6 _____   7+ _____   Have not met _____

2. What rating best describes your feelings about these meetings?
   Scale: 1 (most negative) to 10 (most positive).

Most negative (–)	1	2	3	4	5	6	7	8	9	10	Most positive (+)
Unproductive											Productive
Nontask oriented											Task oriented
Not well facilitated											Well facilitated
Incompatible group members											Compatible group members
Less than honest communications											Honest communications

3. What, if any, are the positive impacts of these meetings on you personally?

4. What, if any, are the negative impacts or concerns you have had with the learning team meetings?

5. Rate the benefit of participating on a learning team.
   Scale: 1 (not much benefit) to 5 (a great deal of benefit).

To what extent have you gained . . .   *Circle choice.*

New knowledge about teaching and learning?	1	2	3	4	5
New insights about how to reach certain students?	1	2	3	4	5
New ideas about how to improve the way you teach?	1	2	3	4	5
New perspectives on your strengths and weaknesses in teaching?	1	2	3	4	5
A new outlet for expressing and sharing frustrations, concerns, or problems with teaching?	1	2	3	4	5
Greater confidence in using a wider range of instructional and assessment methods?	1	2	3	4	5
A stronger sense of connection or support from other teachers?	1	2	3	4	5
A greater sense of yourself as a professional?	1	2	3	4	5

6. With regard to your selected team focus, how successful has your group been with each activity listed here?
   Scale: 1 (not at all successful) to 5 (extremely successful).

How successful has your learning team been with . . .   *Circle choice.*

Analyzing and discussing student needs?	1	2	3	4	5
Reading research and studying successful strategies for addressing student needs and discussing applications of what we have read/studied?	1	2	3	4	5
Discussing similarities and differences in teachers' approaches and beliefs about teaching?	1	2	3	4	5
Investigating programs, strategies, and materials that might help motivate students?	1	2	3	4	5
Designing new materials, lessons, or assessments for students?	1	2	3	4	5
Trying out new techniques, materials, or approaches in teaching and assessing students?	1	2	3	4	5
Sharing successful strategies you currently use?	1	2	3	4	5
Assessing and sharing results of new approaches to teaching with the learning team?	1	2	3	4	5

(Continued)

Handout 3.3 (Continued)

7. Of the teachers on your learning team, how many do you think believe the learning team approach has significant potential to help teachers improve students' motivation and performance? _____ *(give number)*

8. Below is a list of activities that support teacher growth and development. Try to assess the activities in terms of whether they were practiced effectively at the school before the learning teams began.
   Scale: 1 (not very effectively practiced) to 5 (very effectively practiced) before the learning teams began.

Circle choice.

Teachers talked to each other about how they taught and the results they got.	1	2	3	4	5
Teachers learned from each other by watching each other teach.	1	2	3	4	5
Teachers designed lessons, assessments, or units together.	1	2	3	4	5
Teachers critiqued lessons, assessments, or units for each other.	1	2	3	4	5
Teachers reviewed the curriculum across grade levels in a particular subject.	1	2	3	4	5
Teachers developed interdisciplinary strategies to increase student interest and learning.	1	2	3	4	5
Teachers shared articles and other professional resources and read and discussed books.	1	2	3	4	5
Teachers asked each other for advice and help with particular students and topics.	1	2	3	4	5
Teachers visited other schools to examine instructional approaches in other settings.	1	2	3	4	5
Teachers worked together to examine student classroom tests and other student work samples to better understand student strengths and weaknesses.	1	2	3	4	5
Teachers provided moral support and encouragement to each other in trying new ideas.	1	2	3	4	5
Teachers helped each other implement ideas from workshops they attended.	1	2	3	4	5

9. In your opinion, what percentage of your students have benefited from your learning team participation?

   Less than 25%_____   26–50% _____   51–75% _____   76% + _____

10. Indicate your level of agreement with each of the following statements based on your experiences so far with the learning team.
    Scale: 1 (not at all) to 5 (a great deal).

I think my participation on the learning team will . . .   *Circle choice.*

Improve my overall teaching effectiveness.	1	2	3	4	5
Improve my skills in helping students learn.	1	2	3	4	5
Change my perceptions about some students' learning abilities.	1	2	3	4	5
Increase my understanding of how to motivate students to work harder.	1	2	3	4	5
Significantly change how I teach.	1	2	3	4	5
Significantly change how I work with other teachers.	1	2	3	4	5

11. Indicate your level of agreement with each of the following statements.
    Scale: 1 (strongly disagree) to 5 (strongly agree).

Circle choice.

I am enthusiastic about my participation on a learning team.	1	2	3	4	5
I feel a lot of stress during the workday.	1	2	3	4	5
I need more time for learning team participation.	1	2	3	4	5
I am satisfied with my work environment here.	1	2	3	4	5
I am excited by my students' accomplishments this year.	1	2	3	4	5
Student motivation is a major problem here.	1	2	3	4	5
Teachers here tend to do their own thing in the classroom with little coordination.	1	2	3	4	5
I often feel unsure of my teaching.	1	2	3	4	5
Teachers here get along well.	1	2	3	4	5

SOURCE: Reprinted with permission from *A Facilitator's Guide to Professional Learning Teams,* Greensboro, NC: SERVE, 2005.

HANDOUT 3.4: TEAM MEETINGS

Remember, you can personalize this to meet the needs of your team.

We start our meetings on time.

    Never   **1**   **2**   **3**   **4**   **5**   **6**   **7**   **Always**

We review and develop the meeting's agenda/goal before the meeting begins.

    Never   **1**   **2**   **3**   **4**   **5**   **6**   **7**   **Always**

We set time limits for the meeting.

    Never   **1**   **2**   **3**   **4**   **5**   **6**   **7**   **Always**

We identify a recorder to compile notes of the meeting.

    Never   **1**   **2**   **3**   **4**   **5**   **6**   **7**   **Always**

We encourage participation by all members.

    Never   **1**   **2**   **3**   **4**   **5**   **6**   **7**   **Always**

We summarize what we have accomplished in each meeting before concluding the meeting.

    Never   **1**   **2**   **3**   **4**   **5**   **6**   **7**   **Always**

We briefly evaluate each meeting in terms of efficient, productive use of time and each member's concerns.

    Never   **1**   **2**   **3**   **4**   **5**   **6**   **7**   **Always**

We end our meetings on time.

    Never   **1**   **2**   **3**   **4**   **5**   **6**   **7**   **Always**

SOURCE: Reprinted with permission from *Tools for Schools*, April/May 2001.

4

Making
Decisions

The group was fairly new, and members had barely begun their third meeting when they came to an action item on the agenda they had set for themselves. They had an overarching goal for what they hoped to achieve, and this was the first step in making that goal a reality. But at this point in the meeting, the teamwork broke down.

The outside observer intervened, pointing out that the group had not followed several guidelines for making decisions and might do better on the next action item by doing so. She suggested the group determine *who* should make the next decision and *how*. Group members listened thoughtfully to her comments.

At the next action item on the agenda, the group leader stepped up to a flip chart and asked members to identify specifically what issue was being decided. After a few hesitant starts, the comments revealed differences of opinion as to exactly what was being decided. The group sorted out its thoughts until members had a clear statement of the decision before them. The group discussed whether all members needed to be involved in making the decision and agreed they should. They also agreed to abide by a consensus process.

The leader then asked group members for any data or research related to the decision and made sure that each member had an opportunity to present a point of view, which she recorded on the chart paper. She next asked members to assume the roles of different stakeholders to debate the issue as the group weighed the pros and cons of the choices they had discussed.

Finally, the group discussed a final action on the agenda item and came to an agreement.

This time, members' body language was much more open and relaxed. People seemed more alert and attentive, facing the leader and each other. The tension in the room was broken.

Making decisions is not an easy task for a collection of individual thinkers, but it is at the heart of group work. While any one decision may not have a significant impact, the group's collective decision-making ability determines its effectiveness.

The group leader or facilitator plays an important role in ensuring that the group takes an organized approach to decision making and is clear about who makes the decision and the process to be used. Most action items require that the group clarify the issue and decide on a process for making the decision, and groups benefit from spending time to be sure members understand the decision and the process they will use to make the decision before them. Groups facing a significant action item may want to follow this process. Depending on the complexity of the issue and the group's clarity, the time involved will vary.

REVIEW *WHAT* WILL BE DECIDED

The leader asks the group to state clearly *what* is being decided, including the need upon which the action is based and the expected outcome or result of the action being discussed. For example, a group member might say,

> Based on standardized testing data showing that this year's third-grade students are not performing well on reading comprehension, we would like to ask a small group of second- and third-grade teachers to review past standardized performance data and grade-level assessments pertaining to comprehension and use the data to determine whether there is a pattern or trend. We would like this small group to review current research on best practices related to teaching comprehension skills to early readers and bring suggestions back to the full team. When we have reviewed that information, we will take the next step in deciding our approach to this problem.

Being specific about what is being acted on now and what is not will help clarify expectations for everyone in the room and diminish confusion and failed expectations.

DETERMINE *WHO* WILL DECIDE

Some groups may include individuals who all are "on the same page," with similar philosophies, problem-solving approaches, and roles or power. More common, however, are groups made up of people who vary in background, skill, and roles or power.

Since many conflicts result from disagreements about power and authority, groups with a clear understanding of who has decision-making authority will have fewer conflicts. It is important for the group leader or facilitator to work with group members to determine *who* gets to make decisions. High-performing teams learn to negotiate and clearly define the most appropriate decision-making approach for each situation. Decisions can be made differently, depending on the situation. Some decisions may best be made by one person. Time and who will ultimately be accountable for the outcome of the action are key factors in deciding who should make decisions. Some styles are discussed in the following section.

Autocratic

A leader makes the decision alone, relying on personal experience and available information. This individual may obtain information from others and use the information to make the decision, but he or she is accountable for the decision. After making the decision, this individual accepts the responsibility to inform others of the decision.

Autocratic decisions are appropriate in the following situations:

• *A decision must be made immediately in an emergency or crisis.* If there is a fire or a student is injured, the individual at the scene isn't going to call a team together to decide what to do. In these cases, an individual must take responsibility and do what needs to be done. The key, however, is for individuals to use good judgment about what constitutes an emergency. Time is the critical variable, and the decision maker must factor in how limited the time really is before making a unilateral decision.

In one example, a superintendent called a principal to inform him the local college president was on his way over to discuss a proposed pilot project. The college president was looking for a high school to implement a university initiative, and the superintendent was asking this principal to make a decision on whether to volunteer. The superintendent put the principal on the spot in the phone call, and the principal said yes. His staff was furious. The staff viewed this situation as a critical decision, and the principal would have been better off had he asked the superintendent if he could call him back in 15 minutes, to give him time to poll key members of the staff. His staff might have been more understanding of the "crisis" if the principal had not routinely used an autocratic decision-making process. In this case, the union president was called in, and the relationship between the principal and staff spiraled down because of too much autocracy. It also, of course, impacted the university partnership.

An example in which an autocratic decision worked is one where a group leader was notified by a state department of education official that $13,000 remained in a grant that another district had not spent but the deadline for spending it was just hours away. Filling out the requisition paperwork alone would take most of the time. Did this person call the team together to debate the priorities? She did not. She completed the paperwork and made decisions based on the team's past discussions. The team was delighted when she shared the news. Past practice and trust were key to the differences in the two stories.

• *The situation requires confidentiality.* Many decisions have an element of privacy or confidentiality. For example, a principal is going to decide without group discussion whether to renew the contract of a first-year teacher. A superintendent is going to decide whether to accept the resignation of a key staff member based on confidential personnel issues that should not become public. In another case, a district wellness committee wanted a teacher fired. There were many reasons for this, and the motivation for the uprising was a questionable lesson he had introduced to his health students. The superintendent had to use diplomacy to remind the members of the wellness committee that they did not have the authority to hire, fire, or supervise staff. The superintendent accepted the feedback from the committee as advisory and during the process clarified the role and purpose of the team.

• *The decision affects only the decision maker.* An individual doesn't need to bring decisions to the team that affect only the individual, such as whether to apply for a grant to fund a classroom activity or accept a student teacher.

• *The decision maker is accountable for the decision.* If the buck stops at one person's desk, that person needs the authority to make the decision. If the superintendent may be called into court and questioned about a decision, the superintendent rather than a committee or group must have the authority to make the decision.

• *There is a rule or policy that is being implemented.* Autocratic decisions may be made when there is a policy, regulation, or law that has already been established and the leader is merely implementing the decision. It is important to be clear with the staff when sharing this type of decision.

• *The issue does not have a significant impact on others.* Some groups can spend time on truly trivial matters, such as whether the information being handed out should be on blue or yellow paper. In another example, a group responsible for the layout of the school's parent newsletter could never agree on which article should be first. In these cases, the group should give the decision to one person and support that person's decision even if others would have made different choices, because ultimately, it really doesn't matter that much. Think of the cost of the team's time spent on an issue.

There are many times when it is appropriate to make an autocratic decision. The key is to use it wisely and be clear about the authority of the decision when it is shared with others.

Consultative

Using a consultative method of decision making, the leader shares the problem with others individually or collectively and solicits others' ideas or suggestions before making a decision. The decision may or may not reflect their input. The leader generally retains the authority for the final decision and is accountable for the decision.

Consultative decisions are appropriate in the following situations:

- *The issue is likely to generate diverse opinions.* For example, if a school has to install portable classrooms, the school leader may need to make the final decision about which class will be moved to the portable. Each grade-level team in that case might have a different suggestion. The school leader will want the staff's input but ultimately must be responsible for the choice. Scheduling is a similar situation. If these decisions were made by a majority vote, for example, the largest team might have undue weight. By soliciting opinions on a consultative basis, the decision maker honors others' opinions but takes responsibility for the final selection.

- *Some details are confidential.* Sometimes the individual in authority can relate only part of the story but would still find input valuable in making a decision. The leader might present possible solutions to scenarios without providing specific details. For example, a decision maker might want input into some personnel decisions or handling a sensitive situation, such as a child with a serious illness, but would describe the situation without naming the individuals involved or identifying characteristics.

- *Others will be responsible for implementing the decision.* In the scenario in which the principal made a decision affecting the whole staff in a phone call with the superintendent, the principal could have alleviated the ensuing uproar among staff simply by asking the superintendent for 15 minutes to gather input from three or four people. Although the decision may ultimately rest with one person, those affected would prefer to be involved.

One critical element of this decision-making style is that the person who has the authority to make the decision should always make it clear where the final authority for the decision rests. Often, people who are consulted about a decision misinterpret their involvement, thinking think that because they made certain suggestions, their proposals will be the final solutions. The leader may say something like, "I value your opinion and yet want you to understand that there are very diverse ideas about this topic. Please understand that I will talk to a wide variety of people and gather different perspectives before I make the final decision."

Majority Rules/Percentage Vote

A fast, straightforward process is the traditional "vote." The group shares and discusses the issue. Majority rules and percentage vote are processes that everyone is familiar with. They follow our democratic rule. Everyone has one vote, and everyone understands that the minority will accept the will of the majority. Voting by majority rules or percentage vote works when the group agrees to accept the decision of the whole.

Voting is quick and efficient, but it sometimes creates a win-lose situation and tends not to gain the support of the whole group for the decision. There are several different ways to organize a simple voting process, including a simple majority, a quorum, or a specified percentage of members. Members using these methods should discuss the number of votes needed to pass an action.

One type of vote allows a *simple majority:* half plus one. A simple majority is best used only in lower-impact decisions. It allows for a lot of residual negativity among the many who did not vote for the winning option. For example, a 51/49 split results in a significant amount of dissension during the implementation process.

Quorums are sometimes set to determine how many people must be present before a vote can be taken. During the process, teams also decide whether there can be a vote cast if someone is not present at the meeting or whether someone can vote by proxy for another member of the team.

A *percentage vote* can set a higher bar. Many groups ask for a consent vote of between 66% and 80%. Because any group is likely to have 17% of individuals who can be categorized as resisters (Rogers & Rogers, 2003), setting a requirement of any higher than 80% makes a positive outcome hard to achieve. I often use 70% for a percentage vote. There is generally a discussion about the "right" number.

Majority rules or percentage vote decisions are appropriate in the following situations:

- *It is important that every person on the team have a voice in the final decision.* People understand the democratic process, and although some may be resistant, such a process is generally accepted as fair.

- *It is understood that any of the alternatives being considered are acceptable.* If one of the alternatives is not acceptable, the group should not vote. For example, if the principal knows that she will not agree with the staff's decision to implement whole-group instruction in every class, the principal should not allow the group the opportunity to vote on that as an option. If a student group is weighing in on the dress code and proposes halter tops as acceptable attire, a higher-level authority in the school may intervene and remove that from the list of options.

- *The group has little time and it is important to demonstrate the power of the majority.* Voting is a very efficient method. A simple show of hands is often a quick way to check the level of support for an idea. In addition, the data are invaluable. A principal can take a staff vote to the superintendent and say, "We voted, and 83% of our staff support . . ."

- *There is a need for anonymity.* One advantage of majority rules or percentage vote is that the vote can be taken anonymously or publicly. The group leader, facilitator, or at times the group members might want to consider whether some in the group might support an option privately but be unwilling to raise their hands in front of colleagues. If the issue is the least bit sensitive, opt for a private ballot. Be conscious of how group members might feel about a public vote.

After the group has voted, it is important for the team to discuss the method for ensuring that the chosen option is enacted. For example, if staff members have voted to use a lesson study process for professional learning, they may decide that the principal, vice principal, and the department heads must be sure that those who did not support the idea still adhere to the outcome. The principal might say,

> I understand this was really a tough issue for you. However, as a group, we agreed on the democratic process. Let's talk about your options. You can join us. If this action is inconsistent with your personal beliefs, you may want to talk about transferring to a different building. As your supervisor, I hope that won't be your choice, but the implementation of this process is not negotiable. We agreed by a 79% vote that all of our teachers will participate in this approach.

The principal or team leader then must follow up with observations to support the group's action.

Consensus

Consensus is a very popular decision-making strategy, and yet it is often misunderstood or practiced improperly. The definition I use is that *consensus* is reached when each member has had an opportunity to express his or her opinion and all agree to accept, support, and implement the group's decision. A *true consensus decision* is reached when all members of the group are able to clearly state, "I agree to support this decision." I do not call it consensus if members of the group can only say, "I can live with it." Also, groups haven't reached a true consensus if members support a choice because they don't want to spend more time meeting or they agree with the group just to get along. Consensus means that all members understand the issue and agree that they are willing to support the chosen option, even when it may not have been their first choice.

The group should also determine in advance what it will do if consensus cannot be achieved.

Consensus decisions are appropriate in the following situations:

- *When the group is small and members have time to do the work.* Building consensus takes time, to be sure that all members' voices are heard in the process. Because of the time needed to honor each individual, it is hard to use a consensus process in a group larger than 20.

While I have used it in much larger groups, it is an inefficient process with a large group. A group must be willing to commit to consensus decision making, and the leader or facilitator's job is to help the group understand the concept.

- *When buy-in is important for successful implementation.* The group leader or facilitator begins by allowing each group member the opportunity to state his or her concerns about any option. Members discuss what impact each option will have on involved stakeholders. The leader or facilitator often does not take a position during the discussion and ensures that each member has an opportunity to present his or her point of view, as well as any data or research pertinent to the matter before the group.

- *When groupthink is not a preestablished culture. Groupthink* is a phenomenon in which the desire for harmony, a common trait among educators, wins out over the need to express one's dissent or provide contrasting information. Irving Janis, who first identified the concept in 1971, listed symptoms he said contribute to groupthink behavior, many of which develop out of a very unified, cohesive group. In all the discussions, the group leader or facilitator must take care that the most forceful individual or predominant view does not take over the dialogue. The benefits of having a cohesive group are many, but when the group has developed strong ties and an identity, the leader or facilitator must be cautious of groupthink, which can cause the group not to completely and fully analyze alternatives, do research, examine risks, and process information.

- *When the group will make a better decision than any one of the individual members.* The concept of synergy applies when "thrashing through all of the perspectives of team members results in a better solution than what any one, two, or several members might have developed" (Blake & Mouton, 1985, p. 106).

> **Tip:** Group leaders or facilitators must keep in mind that group dynamics often lead people to make decisions based on past experiences or to maintain the status quo and, accordingly, guide the discussion to clarify and avoid such situations.

After preliminary discussions have concluded, the leader or facilitator might encourage people to offer dissenting opinions during a "second chance" time. Another method to be sure that all angles and aspects of the issue are explored is to assign one group member the role of "devil's advocate" to present opposing arguments. Group members must recognize and honor this role, and the group leader or facilitator must be careful to point out the individual's purpose as the role-playing continues, so the group member does not have to remind colleagues continually that he or she may not personally support that position, but is acting to help the group consider other views.

The group leader or facilitator must do regular checks, explicitly testing for consensus at key points. One way to do this is through a consensus voting process. The facilitator can hand each group member a reference sheet. (See Handout 4.1: Consensus Voting.)

HANDOUT 4.1: CONSENSUS VOTING

The facilitator asks individuals to react to a proposal by raising the number of fingers that correspond to their position.

5: I strongly support this idea. I will be a leader.

4: I support this idea. I will provide support.

3: I support this idea. I still have some questions, but I'm willing to trust the group's opinion.

2: I'm not sure. I need more discussion.

1: I can't support the idea it at this time. I need more information.

0: (Fist) No, I cannot support this idea. I have major concerns/reservations. I need an alternative I can support.

SOURCE: Reprinted with permission from *Keys to Successful Meetings*, Oxford, OH: National Staff Development Council, 1994, and reprinted from *Tools for Schools*, February/March 2005.

Tip: There are other simple strategies for taking the pulse of the group or testing for readiness to make a decision. Some groups use "thumbs up," "thumb to the side," or "thumbs down." Others use cards with a red light, yellow light, or green light.

The group continues the discussion until there seems to be a consensus developing. As the group begins to agree on an option, the facilitator or group leader must help members understand what is expected for each level of commitment to a consensus decision (Richardson, 2004). The group leader or facilitator creates a chart with categories labeled "minimal support," "moderate support," "proactive support," and "maximum support." (Use Handout 4.2: Commitment Continuum.) Members define what each level of support looks like. After the group reaches its final decision, the leader or facilitator can remind members that they have chosen to support this final option and to what degree they are committed.

If the group gets stuck at any point, some options are as follows:

• Consider taking a break to reflect and regroup. When group members return, the facilitator or leader can ask each member to state his or her opinion. The leader or facilitator may create a compromise position and ask the group to react to it.

• The leader or facilitator also can create a contradictory statement to refocus the discussion and identify real concerns.

• Use a balance sheet to allow a group to identify and review the pros and cons of a variety of options. Like the other tools for reaching consensus, balance sheets won't make decisions. They will, however, organize the information and facilitate discussion among group members. Balance sheets may look much like force field analysis, but they are quite different in purpose. A balance sheet is a quick way to document the pros and cons of one or more choices. Its purpose is not so much analytical as to move a group closer to a decision. Balance sheets are simpler and quicker to apply than many other tools and may be all that is necessary to spark consensus on either a problem or proposed solution. (See Handout 4.3: Balance Sheet.)

• A final thought if the group still seems to be struggling is to ask another individual to take the role of leader or facilitator. Sometimes a new facilitator will ask the question or guide a dialogue in a new way or may reframe the issue to bring more clarity.

HANDOUT 4.2: COMMITMENT CONTINUUM

Purpose

Display the distribution of agreement with the option and the level of contribution participants are willing to give to implementation of the decision.

Directions

1. On the flip chart or on a transparency, record the option being considered. Facilitate a dialogue to ensure that all participants have a common understanding of the option. *Time: 5 minutes.*
2. Remind the participants that they have reached the group's decision through consensus and now they are identifying their level of commitment to implement this decision. *Time: 5 minutes.*
3. Clarify the meaning of the Levels of Yes and No. *Time: 5 minutes.*
4. Give participants two sticky dots each and ask them to place one of the dots on the number that matches their current level of agreement or disagreement regarding the option. *Time: 5 minutes.*
5. Compute and announce the results indicated by the dots. Again, confirm that most of the participants agree with the option. *Time: 5 minutes.*
6. Review the Levels of Contribution and Support for the option. *Time: 5 minutes.*
7. Invite participants to place their second dot on the number that represents their willingness to support and contribute to the successful implementation of the decision. *Time: 5 minutes.*
8. Debrief the results indicated by the dots. Are there sufficient dots in the maximum and proactive sections to ensure implementation? If not, the team needs to problem solve this situation. It is essential that some team members are willing to lead the implementation and work proactively to successfully implement the decision. Once there are sufficient dots in these two categories, the team's decision is declared and the team can develop its action plan for implementation. *Time: 15 minutes.*

LEVEL OF YES/NO		LEVEL OF CONTRIBUTION AND SUPPORT
Strong agreement *I think this is the* *best option.*	10 9 8	Maximum support *I will lead/facilitate the planning, implementation,* *and evaluation.*
Agreement *I think this is a* *workable option.*	7 6 5	Proactive support *I'll help plan and carry out the comprehensive* *implementation.*
Disagreement *I have some concerns.*	4 3	Moderate support *As an individual, I will look for things I can do to* *support implementation.*
Strong disagreement *I think this is a mistake.*	2 1	Minimal support *As an individual, I'll do what is necessary to* *support the decision.*

HANDOUT 4.3: BALANCE SHEET

It is always useful to identify the advantages and disadvantages of each of the options. Some groups prefer to use the language of plusses and minuses or benefits and costs. In some environments, we use pluses and deltas (ideas we'd like to celebrate and suggestions we have for modification or improvement).

Proposed Solution _____

Advantage/Plus/Benefit	**Disadvantage/Minus/Cost**
_____	_____
_____	_____
_____	_____
_____	_____
_____	_____
_____	_____
_____	_____
_____	_____
_____	_____
_____	_____
_____	_____
_____	_____

> **Tips for Building Consensus**
>
> - Think of consensus as win-win, not compromise.
> - At key decision points, combat the illusion of consensus—explicitly test for it using one of the voting methods discussed in this chapter or use a straw vote.
> - Stamp out the declaration "I can live with it."
> - Develop shared values regarding decision making.
> - Encourage flexibility: Explode the mind-set that consensus is all-or-nothing.
> - When no choice stands out, start the discussion with the alternative that has the least opposition.
> - When differences are numerous or complex, work through the issues one step at a time.
> - Take breaks. Call time-out to reflect and regroup.
> - When consensus seems unachievable, form a smaller group to create consensus that can be used as a springboard to consensus within the whole group.
> - Seek conditional consensus if the group is polarized, getting support to try an option for a set period of time.
> - When the group gets stuck, back up and try again.
> - Move ahead with another decision-making process when consensus is not possible.

I once did some work in a school district that had guidelines for shared decision making. The rule was "All decisions will be made by consensus. If consensus cannot be reached, there will be no decision." Stop and read that rule again. If every individual in the group did not agree, nothing happened. And so the district struggled with many examples of stalled action because it is not always possible to achieve consensus, especially in a large or diverse group.

Consensus is a worthy goal, but I am cautious about using it because it means that every person must support the decision. In a strategic-planning group of 30 people in another location, a small group of 3 people who shared a similar personal philosophy banded together, and that group blocked the process consistently. Is it reasonable to allow 3 people in the minority to stop the process that 27 representatives agree on?

The Will of the Group

Sometimes, a feasible alternative is to agree to honor the "will of the group." The will of the group is a modification of consensus that allows the group to work through the discussion and narrowing process. The definition of "will of the group," according to Eaker, DuFour, and DuFour (2002), is that "all members agree that they will have arrived at a decision when all points of view have been heard and the will of the group is evident *even to all who oppose it*" (p. 94).

Will-of-the-group decisions are appropriate in the following situations:

- *If 33 people are in a group and 29 people in the group agree on an action and 4 people do not, the will of the group is fairly evident.* The facilitator or group leader's role is to be sure that each person has had the opportunity to be heard and to explain his or her position and it is agreed that the minority group cannot hold up the process. Some may be tempted to set a percentage approval in this process, but setting a required number is more similar to a traditional vote than to the will of the group. In honoring the will of the group, the members agree that they will support the group in implementing the decision despite having a dissimilar views. Everyone's opinion is acknowledged, and all agree that they support the process moving forward.

- *Change research is clear.* The literature on change notes that in any group, 8% will be innovators, 17% will be leaders, 29% will be early adopters, 29% will be late adopters, and 17% will be resisters (Rogers & Rogers, 2003). On the face of it, that seems to make it more likely that a group can recognize a majority will rather than reach full consensus.

- *There is time, and the size of the group is manageable.* Group leaders and facilitators need to allow time with this approach, just as with consensus, for each group member to be heard. Because of that, the larger the size of the group, the less feasible the process.

Groups with decision-making authority may determine that their final action will be decided by consensus, by will of the group, or through voting. The facilitator or group leader should involve the group in reviewing the means of making a decision and have the group determine how it would like to proceed before getting to the point of taking action.

While I hold to a strict definition of consensus, I have worked with groups that use a more liberal definition. The leader or facilitator may begin by having each group member define what will determine consensus and having the group discuss members' perceptions. The leader or facilitator asks each group member to write a definition for consensus. When all are done, individuals form groups of three to share definitions and merge their thoughts into one piece. When the groups have completed the task, they merge into groups of six and repeat the assignment. When two groups remain, the whole group comes together. The leader posts the definitions and facilitates a discussion that will lead to a consensus decision. Reaching agreement on the definition of consensus is good practice if a group plans to use this decision-making process.

Use A.R.C.I.O. to Help

A helpful first step sometimes is to identify who currently is responsible for decisions and review past actions according to a A.R.C.I.O. chart. Each letter of the acronym is used to fill in the cells of a chart: consult, out of the loop, inform, responsible for, and approve. (See Handout 4.4: A.R.C.I.O. for a form to use.)

HANDOUT 4.4: A.R.C.I.O.

Directions

First, identify the groups that need to be in your top cells. The example here will provide ideas. Revise the top row to include the real groups and titles used in your school or district. For each action issue listed in the left margin, members fill in the appropriate cell with one of the following letters:

A for Approve. Who needs to approve the decision? (There may be more than one A.)
R for Responsible. Who is responsible for making and implementing the decision?
C for Consult. Who needs to be consulted before the decision is made?
I for Inform. Who needs to be told about the decision?
O for Out of the Loop. These are individuals or groups who do not need to be consulted.

Sample Decision-Making Matrix: *Who Gets to Make What Decisions*

Issues	Givens (board policy, contracts, regulations)	Supt./ Central Office	Principal	School Improvement Team	Grade Level/ Dept. Chairs	Committees	Staff	Parents	Students	Other

Teams or small groups identify a handful of major decisions in the school or district. The tasks are written in the first cell of each row. Across the top of the chart are cells indicating different stakeholders. As the group looks at each stakeholder group's involvement in each task, members can discuss ways to improve decision making and the most efficient and collaborative methods.

In one middle school, three teachers took issue with the principal's decisions about room assignments. The principal decided to give responsibility for the room assignments to a committee of teachers. She handed over the building layout with the number of rooms, a list of the class sections, the assignments of students with individual education plans, and the teacher list—all the data for making the decisions. The committee moved the R in the chart to a committee of teachers acknowledging that the committee was responsible for the decision. They would consult with the principal and the teachers, and therefore they both got Cs on the chart. And they agreed that the teachers would all be informed by the committee when the decision was made, so the teachers were also recognized with an I. Three weeks later, the teachers came back in and asked the principal to make the final decision about the room assignments. Their friends weren't happy with the decisions they were making, and they were being shunned in the teachers' lounge. Reviewing who had the responsibility and allowing it to shift ultimately helped everyone agree on who should make the final selection.

DETERMINE *HOW* DECISIONS WILL BE MADE

By determining who is making the decision, the group can move on to *how* the decision is to be made. There are a variety of tools that can be used to help the facilitator and the team collect valuable data and insights about the group's thinking. Some of these tools might help you and your groups.

A thorough outline and discussion before calling for action will make the process move forward more smoothly and make the ensuing commitment of the group to the decision much firmer. If the group has clarified the decision to be made, is clear about roles and responsibilities, and has clearly chosen a method by which the decision will be made, it is time to take action. Again, not every decision requires the thoroughness described here, but major decisions that involve significant outcomes do. A group would not follow these steps to decide where to meet, for example, but would do so in choosing district goals for a strategic plan. Whether by consensus or vote, the group is ready now to determine its course and next moves.

If group members want to narrow their options, several tools are possible. List reduction, dots, weighted voting, nominal group process, criteria rating forms, and paired comparisons are helpful when the group has identified many possible options and must narrow the selection, such as in hiring, adopting textbooks, or strategizing responses to an identified concern. Each method provides a variety of ways for groups to decide between and among many choices.

Weighted voting gives each member a number of votes to cast to help clarify the group's position on favored actions. *Nominal group process* is a numbered ranking of each item, with each item then prioritized according to its overall group score. In *criteria rating,* group members first identify key criteria for evaluating the options, then cast votes that are weighted according to how important the group has decided each characteristic is. *Paired comparisons* have group members choose one of two options in a series of pairs that match every possibility, until the group determines which option is favored. These tools will provide processes for quickly gathering data and insights about the member's preferences and choices when there are multiple options.

Brainstorm

In many situations, the group leader or facilitator may begin with a brainstorming session to generate alternatives for the group to reach its desired outcome. This is the stage of *divergent thinking,* an opportunity to identify possibilities or create multiple pathways. Brainstorming is a technique designed to generate many ideas in response to a question or problem (see Handout 4.5: Brainstorming). Brainstorming is an idea-generating technique pioneered by Alex Osborn, an advertising executive. Members of a group spontaneously express their ideas as they think of them, so that each has the opportunity to build on the ideas of others. Brainstorming results can be improved by asking participants to consider adapting, modifying, magnifying, substituting, rearranging, reversing, combining, or otherwise changing ideas that have been presented.

Brainstorming

The facilitator reviews these basic rules of brainstorming with the group:

- Suspend all judgment.
- Say each idea out loud as it occurs to you.
- Hitchhike or "piggyback" on others' ideas.
- Encourage a free, uninterrupted flow of ideas.
- Be outrageous.
- Record all ideas.

The team leader presents a problem for which ideas are sought. The wording of the problem should encourage specific, tangible ideas, not abstract ideas or opinions. The facilitator should make sure that the participants understand the problem, the objective of the brainstorming

HANDOUT 4.5: BRAINSTORMING

Comments to the Facilitator

Brainstorming is a method for tapping the resources of the entire group. Through brainstorming, a group strives for quantity of ideas, not quality. To ensure that that happens, the facilitator asks participants at the beginning to refrain from evaluating or criticizing ideas when they are announced.

Preparation

Post chart paper on a wall where it can be seen clearly by all participants. Distribute sticky notepaper and writing tools.

Directions

1. Identify the topic. Write the topic on chart paper or a chalkboard at the front of the room.

2. Ask each participant to silently write as many issues, concerns, and problems for that topic as they can, using a separate sticky note for each idea. Allow five minutes of thinking/writing time.

3. In sequence, each participant shares one idea aloud with the group. Write each issue, concern, or problem on the chart paper.

4. If an idea is unclear, allow participants to ask for clarification. The participant who suggested the issue, concern, or problem should rewrite the idea on another sticky note, using language that is more clear to everyone.

5. When the group runs out of ideas, use prompts to elicit more suggestions. If more are suggested, add those to the list on the chart paper.

6. With the group's permission, the facilitator should then organize the suggestions into larger categories of concern.

7. The facilitator should address how those concerns will be included in the sessions.

SOURCE: Reprinted with permission from *Tools for Schools*, February/March 2005.

session, and the rules. Regardless of the method used, the output of the brainstorming session must be reviewed and evaluated. List reduction, weighted voting, paired comparisons, and other tools can be used to review the ideas generated by the group.

Group members think aloud, verbalizing their ideas as they occur. Creative ideas multiply during brainstorming and can lead to an imaginative solution to a problem. Brainstorming is helpful when the group wants original or a large number of ideas, when a shift in thinking is required, when the current type or depth of thinking will not lead to the desired results, when time is limited, and when viewing an idea through many perspectives is critical. Asking participants to SCAMPER, that is substitute, combine, adapt, modify or magnify, put to other uses, eliminate or minify, rearrange or reverse, or otherwise change ideas that have been presented can improve brainstorming results (Michalko, 1991, pp. 72–73.)

> **Tip:** To ensure all group members actively participate, control the size of the group.

There are several types of brainstorming. *Freewheeling* is the most familiar type. Group members call out ideas spontaneously, and a scribe records the ideas as they are suggested. The scribe is careful to use the words of the participants and does not translate ideas that have been presented. This method tends to be spontaneous and creative, and it allows participants to build on each other's ideas. Strong individuals may dominate the session, and confusion may set in when people talk at once. If the group is large, the facilitator can divide the large group into smaller groups of five to eight, with a recorder in each group. The recorders write all ideas, as close to the original words of the speaker as possible, on large sheets of chart paper. A timekeeper periodically alerts the groups to the time remaining. When time is up, each group can gather to listen as recorders take turns reading and clarifying the ideas generated.

> **Tip:** The process works best if group members are equal in status and willing to actively participate.

In *round-robin brainstorming*, the scribe asks each member, in turn, for an idea. Members may pass on any round, and the session continues until all members have passed during the round. All ideas are recorded. This ensures that everyone participates in the process but may place some pressure on individuals to come up with ideas every time. In the round-robin method, it is sometimes difficult to wait one's turn, and some may find it difficult to pass.

A larger group may use *carousel brainstorming*. The facilitator records a question or topic for input at the top of chart paper, typically ending up with many pieces of chart paper, each with a different topic or question that requires elaboration. The facilitator posts the charts around the room so that small groups have room to gather around each sheet. Participants count off by the number of charts on the wall. The facilitator sends each group to a different chart, providing each with a different-colored marker. The facilitator announces the amount of time the group will spend brainstorming. When the time is up, the facilitator asks each group to take its marker and move clockwise to the next chart. The group repeats the process and adds to the brainstorming completed by the previous group. The facilitator may choose to decrease the amount of time spent at each chart as groups fill up the charts and begin to run short of ideas. When each group has responded to all questions, the groups read the ideas others have added to their original charts.

The *slip method of brainstorming* is very different. The leader asks members to write down their ideas on sticky notes or index cards. The ideas are posted on the wall, and the leader asks participants to group or organize the ideas. Since the opportunity to build creatively on other ideas as the lists are generated is reduced in this method, it is important to remind participants to bring their sticky notes to the wall when they are organizing the ideas so they can continue to write ideas throughout the process. This allows for some opportunity to build on the ideas of others. This format allows the participants to move to the next step of organizing, grouping, and prioritizing more easily than in the other methods.

When the group has a list of possible solutions, members may need to narrow their options to be able to make a final selection from the most desirable.

Narrow the Choices

Groups sometimes use more than one method to narrow their selections when they have identified many wonderful options (and maybe some crazy ones). For example, some groups might begin with dots, to narrow a long list to a more manageable list of five or six choices, and then do a weighted comparison or paired comparison. Or the group might want to set criteria to evaluate the remaining choices using the criteria rating form. Applying criteria can help all members focus on the group's priorities and come closer to reaching a decision. There are several methods of narrowing options.

List Reduction

List reduction is a method of processing all the ideas generated during a brainstorming session. It is critical before you begin list reduction to clarify the options, so all members understand them, and then to reduce the options to a manageable number.

Before the list of potential problems or solutions can be shortened, everyone in the group must have a clear understanding of all the items on the list. The facilitator should review each item on the list to see whether there is a need for clarification. If an item needs to be explained, the person who made the suggestion should be the one to clarify. The discussion should not go beyond a simple clarification.

The group may then choose to combine similar ideas by clustering them under one heading. No ideas should ever be crossed out or eliminated, to ensure that no one feels that his or her ideas are not valued by the group. Listing each idea allows group members to review ideas later, if necessary. Ideas can be bracketed when they are combined.

The group may begin to reduce the list by establishing criteria to screen the ideas. The criteria, called *filters,* for selecting solutions include the following:

- Is this solution likely to solve the problem?
- Is it feasible?
- Can we afford it?

Don't rule out solutions based on cost alone, because some additional brainstorming may yield ideas for finding resources or completing the project for less money.

When using list reduction earlier in the process, some filters for selecting problems are as follows:

- Does this problem lend itself to being solved by a group?
- Is this problem within our control or influence?
- Is it worth solving?

Keeping the filters in mind, group members vote on each item on the list. A simple majority can keep an item on the list. Any group member can keep an item on the list if the person asks the group to learn more about the idea before deciding not to consider it. Again, do not cross items out. Use brackets to reduce the list of ideas.

In general, the group focuses on and continues to evaluate only the ideas that are not bracketed. The process may be repeated with more or less stringent filters until the list is reduced to approximately six options, a manageable number that can then be evaluated using some of the other tools listed below.

Weighted Voting

Weighted voting is often used on the way to consensus decision making and is a way to quantify group members' positions and preferences. This is most useful for "taking the temperature" of the group as it is working toward consensus and provides information about where individuals stand and how strongly they feel about an issue. This approach can help surface opposing view-

> **Tip:** Weighted voting is best used when fewer than eight options are being considered.

points and priorities that may prevent the group from reaching consensus. Weighted voting should not be used to make the final decision.

The leader or facilitator draws a grid on a flip chart, showing "group members" on the vertical axis and "options" on the horizontal axis. Each individual has a set number of votes to cast. One rule of thumb is to allow each person a number of votes equal to 1.5 times the total number of options. Each member then indicates his or her preferences among the existing options. The group does not use any criteria for deciding among the options, nor do members discuss the benefits and drawbacks of any of the options or attempt to agree on a single option. The leader should encourage group members to represent their feelings about the options and not cast all their votes on a single favorite. Members write down their votes, which afterward are recorded on the chart. By writing them down rather than expressing them verbally in turn, the leader or facilitator prevents groupthink from influencing individuals' choices. The leader asks for and records votes by option and records the votes for the group to see where there is agreement.

An example is shown in Handout 4.6: Weighted Voting Format. A school team is trying to decide how to spend a $20,000 grant and has identified four ways to spend the money. Each member is allowed six votes (1.5 multiplied by the total number of options).

After using the weighted vote to determine the group's priorities, members may begin a discussion to reach consensus or take a final vote based on the top options. Discussion is an important follow-up to this process since it was not a part of the initial vote. It is important to discuss any items with a "0" vote or a high number of points. Preference becomes obvious when the data are gathered.

Nominal Group Process

Nominal group process is a simple ranking similar to using dots, but with a numbered system. When selecting which problem to solve or which option to use, the group may be tempted to listen to the group member who speaks most or has the most authority. The nominal group technique provides a way to give everyone an equal voice in problem solving. The group follows these steps:

1. Have everyone on the team write or say the problem or option he or she feels is most important. Record each statement on the flip chart or somewhere visible. (Writing the issues may protect people who do not feel comfortable speaking up.)

2. Check with the team to make sure there is no repetition. Label each item on the list, beginning with the letter A.

3. Ask group members to write the letters on a piece of paper. If the group had five problems, members would write down the letters A through E.

4. Each person then ranks the items, with the most important receiving the highest number of points. For example, with five items, the preferred item would receive a 5, the next would rate a 4, and so on. The group leader or facilitator collects the rankings and totals each item. The item with the most points is considered first.

5. If the list of items is long, allow group members to select and order only as many items as half the total plus one. For example, in a list of 20 items, each person would rank order 11.

HANDOUT 4.6: WEIGHTED VOTING FORMAT

Weighted voting is a way to quantify the positions and preferences of group members. Weighted voting is most useful for "taking the temperature" of the group as it is working toward consensus. The approach can be used to identify the group's positions and priorities when fewer than eight or ten options are under consideration. No criteria are used. Individual members' votes are recorded; there is no discussion or effort to reach agreement on a single number.

How to Use Weighted Voting

Set up a grid on a flip chart—team members on the vertical axis and options on the horizontal axis. Give each member a number of votes to distribute in accordance with their preferences. (As a rule of thumb, the number of votes should be 1½ times the number of options.) Members then decide how to distribute their votes among the options, to indicate their relative preferences.

Encourage people to spread their votes to represent their relative feelings about the options, rather than lump all their votes on a single favorite. Have members write down how they will distribute their votes before any votes are recorded on the chart. Ask for and record votes by option, not by person. Record all votes so that the group can see where the agreements and disagreements lie.

The data from the weighted voting is not used to make the final decision. It merely gives the group information about where individual members stand and how strongly they feel. This information makes it easier to surface opposing viewpoints. Consensus cannot be reached without addressing those view-points.

Here's an example used by a house team trying to reach consensus on four ways to spend a $20,000 grant. Each member had six votes to distribute.

	A	B	C	D
Sam	1	2	2	1
Susan	2	0	3	1
Patrick	3	1	1	1
Alaina	3	1	1	1
Michael	1	1	2	2
TOTALS:	10	5	9	6

A: A Reading Tutor

B: Musical Instruments

C: Equipment for the Science Lab

D: Field Trips

(Continued)

Handout 4.6 (Continued)

Names/Options	A: A Reading Tutor	B: Musical Instruments	C: Equipment for the Science Lab	D: Field Trips
Sam	1	2	2	1
Susan	2	0	3	1
Patrick	3	1	1	1
Alaina	3	1	1	1
Michael	1	1	2	2
Totals:	**10**	**5**	**9**	**6**

For example, if the group identified *space, safety, hiring, diversity,* and *curriculum* as the critical issues, the facilitator would put up a chart or write the issues on the board with a letter by each: A. space; B. safety; C. hiring; D. diversity; and E. curriculum. Next, each group member would write the letters down on a piece of paper:

A. _____ B. _____ C. _____ D. _____ E. _____

If a person thought safety was most important, he or she would write the number 5 on the line after the item for B. Another person might consider safety to be second in importance and would write the number 4. Each person completes the list.

The facilitator gathers the rankings on the flip chart or other visual aid as shown:

A. 2, 5, 2, 4, 1 = 14

B. 1, 4, 5, 5, 5 = 20

C. 4, 1, 3, 3, 4 = 15

D. 5, 2, 1, 1, 2 = 11

E. 3, 3, 4, 2, 3 = 15

The facilitator adds up each line of numbers. The item with the highest number is the most important to the group as a whole. In this example, safety is the most important item, with a total of 20. The items are rank ordered, and the group begins to address each in order of importance. The data provide an opportunity for the group to discuss the issue with more clarity now. In this example, while four people rated safety as most important or second most important, one person rated it as least important. The data generated through the nominal process technique provide an opening for the conversation about priorities.

Criteria Rating Form

Another very useful tool is the *criteria rating form*. It helps individuals and groups decide the best option or options among a group of options. In problem-solving groups, criteria rating is often used for making complex decisions. It is a more thorough decision-making process than weighted voting, paired comparisons, nominal group process, or even dots. It is like the other tools in that it should be used to collect data and stimulate discussion rather than make a definitive decision, especially if the ratings are close. Criteria rating can be used whenever multiple perspectives and multiple factors affect the options and the decision.

In criteria rating, group members identify the criteria against which they will measure the options. The group sets a rating scale, then creates a template and weights each category to reflect its relative importance to group members. Individuals then rate the options, which are multiplied by the weight. The totals for each category then can be used to stimulate a discussion.

Tip: Weighted voting, nominal process, paired comparison, and criteria rating generally are not used to determine a final action, but to help in narrowing options.

Teams often use criteria rating forms when selecting a candidate for a position or selecting new materials or textbooks. In these scenarios, the group first would identify the possible candidates or options. In the case of an interview team, the district or school likely would have a process in place to review the applications and narrow the list of applicants. Once the top candidates were identified, the group would list the names at the top of a grid and then during the interview or site visitation process, the interviewing committee would assess each candidate against each criterion. Criteria for a principal selection committee might include the following:

- Loves children
- Clear vision
- Experience
- Communication skills
- Experience with supervision of staff
- Demonstrated ability to work with parents
- Experience with curriculum and instruction
- Excellent references
- Writing sample

In the case of a textbook committee, the names of publishers of texts being considered would be listed across the top of the grid, and the criteria might include the following:

- Alignment with state standards
- Reading level
- Student interest
- Quality of teacher materials
- Respect for diversity in the materials/no bias
- Professional development support for implementation
- Associated workbooks
- Unit/benchmark tests, related assessments
- Cost
- Delivery date

A group hiring a new physics teacher might include certification, type of experience, willingness to be a team member, congruence of classroom management philosophy with our school, love of students, and ability to successfully communicate with parents. It is important the each group take the time to identify the criteria to be used to assess the options. This process is a sophisticated, complex system to produce data for discussion, not a final selection; see Table 4.1 for a blank rating form. (See Handout 4.7: Criteria Sort for a similar, related activity.)

(Text continues on page 146)

Table 4.1 Criteria Rating Form

Criteria and Scale	Weighting	Potential Solutions					
Brainstorm Criteria	.5–2.0						
1 2 3 4							
1 2 3 4							
1 2 3 4							
1 2 3 4							
1 2 3 4							
Total							

HANDOUT 4.7: CRITERIA SORT

Purpose

Establish the criteria that will be used to evaluate the proposed options and apply the criteria to those options.

Directions

1. Invite participants to name the criteria for evaluating the options for their situation. Write those on a flip chart.

   ### Examples of Criteria

   Can be done with existing budget, offers support for teachers who want to differentiate their instruction, or compatible with our existing course textbook and materials.

   > **Definition:**
   >
   > Criteria are standards or rules used to evaluate something.

   (Note: A small group may want to work in pairs for this step; larger groups may want to break down into smaller groups of five or six.)

2. After the group lists possible criteria, give participants nine sticky dots in three different colors. Identify one color for each category and ask participants to label them as follows:

   ### Criteria Weight

   3 = *Critical:* An option must match this criterion if we are to reach our goal.
   2 = *Important:* An option should match this criterion if possible.
   1 = *Would be nice:* An option might meet this criterion but it is not essential.

3. Invite participants to use their dots to place three criteria in each category.

4. Tabulate the results and create new lists of the "critical," "important," and "would be nice" criteria. (The group should discuss any criteria that fall in the gaps between two categories. If necessary, the facilitator may have the group vote again on disputed criteria.)

5. Bring forward the list of options that the group created. Post the list of critical criteria next to the options.

6. Give participants another supply of sticky dots and invite them to label each option as follows:

Criteria Match

5 = Matches the criteria
3 = Somewhat matches the criteria
1 = Does not match the criteria

7. On a flip chart, create a larger version of the chart example below and fill out each square on the chart for each option.

8. Create a list that ranks the options from highest to lowest.

	Option 1: Provide teachers with one hour of daily team time				
Criteria	**Criteria Weight**		**Criteria Match**		**Criteria Total**
Must be done within existing budget	3	×	5	=	15
		×		=	

SOURCE: Reprinted with permission from *Tools for Schools*, April/May 2004. Based on recommendations included in *Putting Sense into Consensus*, VISTA Associates, 1998.

Possible Criteria for Determining Options

Many groups have a tough time determining appropriate criteria against which to assess the options. A number of general criteria can be considered, including the following:

- *Control.* Is this option within the group's control? Is the group in a position to implement the idea?
- *Effectiveness.* To what extent does the option address the issue? How likely is this option to achieve the desired outcome?
- *Satisfaction.* Will this option result in the increased satisfaction of parents, community members, staff, students, central office administrators, or others?
- *Time.* How long will it take to implement this option? Some solutions may take less time than others.
- *Cost.* Are the financial resources available to support the initiative?
- *Research base.* Is there research to support this option?
- *Acceptability.* Will those responsible for implementing the idea accept it?

The group then defines a rating scale, say 1 to 4, with 4 being the most desirable. The rating of 4 may not always be the biggest or the most. For example, if cost is a criterion (and it often is), less expensive is more desirable and so would be a 4, while more costly options would rate a lower score on the scale. The rating scale should be made explicit for each criterion and be clear to anyone using the instrument.

Group members next have to determine whether any of the criteria are more important. For example, a group hiring a new physics teacher might decide that being a team player, love of students, and certification are the most desirable characteristics, while the number of years of experience may be less so. If desired, groups can use simple weights of 0.5 to 2.0 to give relative value to each criterion. In some cases, weighting may not be a factor. When looking at textbooks, the group may decide that the reading level, alignment with state standards, professional development, and unit/benchmark tests are all equally important and so there is no need to differentiate the value of the criteria.

Now that the group has the format, each member rates each option and multiplies the rating by the weight. The weighted ratings of each participant are totaled on each of the options. The team discusses the solutions with the highest totals.

This process is slightly different from weighted voting in that rather than a total number of votes being used as a factor in multiplying to compute a final rating, the factor is a criterion-based rating.

Paired Comparisions

Paired comparisons (sometimes called "forced choice") is another tool to help take the group's pulse. Members weight each option against every other option. The strategy helps the group discuss and organize information.

The group leader or facilitator sets up a grid. (See Handout 4.8: Paired Comparisons Worksheet.) The grid allows for each option (e.g., potential solution) to be compared individually with every other option. In each comparison, each member has only one vote and must decide which of the two alternatives is better. Each person casts a vote in each comparison, even if neither choice seems appealing or if both are very desirable. Votes are recorded and totaled when all possible comparisons have been made.

The number of possible comparisons depends on the number of options. Because the number of comparisons increases rapidly as options increase, it is best to use the paired comparison process when the group is evaluating six or fewer options. To see why, consider that if you have three options, your forced choices will be

1 versus 2;

1 versus 3; and

2 versus 3 (three votes).

With four options, the forced choices are

1 versus 2;

1 versus 3;

1 versus 4;

2 versus 3

2 versus 4; and

3 versus 4 (six votes).

With five options, there are nine votes. At six options, the number of votes increases to 15 different comparisons that need to be made.

The power of paired comparisons comes from the choices it forces group members to make. Even when two alternatives seem equal, members must choose one. Having to make difficult choices often leads people to see advantages—or disadvantages—they may not have noticed before. Paired comparisons can be a time-consuming process, but it is more exact than weighted voting.

The facilitator or leader poses the question and asks for a show of hands of those who prefer the first option of the pair. He or she then subtracts that number from the total number in the group (since everyone in the group must vote for one of the options), to get a total for the second option, and records the votes for each.

HANDOUT 4.8: PAIRED COMPARISONS WORKSHEET

Names/Options	1 vs. 2	1 vs. 3	1 vs. 4	1 vs. 5	2 vs. 3	2 vs. 4	2 vs. 5	3 vs. 4	3 vs. 5	4 vs. 5	Total
1.											
2.											
3.											
4.											
5.											

As with other tools, the option receiving the highest total on the paired comparisons chart does not automatically become the group's decision. The process provides data to aid in decision making. After totaling the votes for each option, the leader or facilitator can have the group discuss the findings. Often, several options will have received very few votes and will obviously be eliminated, and two or three will cluster at the top of the group's preferences. In working toward consensus, the group can focus discussion on the two or three top options. Sometimes, group members rapidly come to a consensus or may choose to use another process to continue examining the remaining options.

> **Tip:** Save the record of the paired comparisons discussion in case the group later needs to revisit the rationale for a decision.

Some groups use one tool (even a simple tool like dots) to reduce many options to the five or six top ideas and then use paired comparisons.

Dots

Dots are so easy to use. They allow group members to create a clear visual of the group's preferences. The facilitator posts chart paper on the walls describing each option. Each group member receives a predetermined number of dots. The facilitator tells group members to place one dot on each sheet next to the options that person prefers, voting for options the individual considers top choices. The facilitator then sorts the list, highlighting the options receiving the most votes. Often, it is clear which issues to move forward in the selection process. For example, six of the options received eight or more dots; four options received three dots; and two options received only one dot. In this case, the six that received most of the dots moved forward for further consideration. This is a simple way to reduce a large list.

I have never been in a group using this process in which there wasn't a clear-cut choice. The benefit of using this method is that most people will end up with a choice that they have supported at some point during the process. Once, I worked with a group in which a few people were unhappy that the only options they wanted had been eliminated. They insisted the process was flawed. The feeling in this group was so clearly contentious that we started again using a different voting method. When we used paired comparisons, the result was the same. Although the few members who disagreed still were not pleased with the outcome, they could not claim the process itself was flawed.

The group has decided how it wants to reach a conclusion. Now the facilitator or group leader must help members with the process.

For many groups, these processes will allow them to make the kinds of decisions they face in their meetings fairly, efficiently, and effectively. As the group develops and the facilitator or leader gains skills in different tools for reaching a final decision, they will find they have practiced most, if not all, of the above methods in their discussions.

Some groups, however, face larger tasks, with broader scopes and consequences. These groups may be called on to make the decisions and then create an action plan to implement them. For both facilitator and group, this new challenge requires an even broader array of skills.

5

Taking Action

O ne key task of more and more groups is *action planning.* Facilitating action planning involves carefully following a planned sequence of steps.

Action planning is simply the group's process for creating solutions. When a standing group is formed with the purpose of addressing an issue or is called upon to create a plan, members must set goals and plan how to meet the goals. The action planning process unifies the vision with the steps for accomplishing that vision. It sets out short-term steps, or *milestones,* for reaching a long-term goal. Action plans help group members understand the tasks they need to complete to achieve the goal, their responsibilities for those tasks, and the costs and benefits of implementing the plan.

Devising a focused action plan can enrich learning for participants and teams. The action committee process helps the leader or facilitator engage team members in a conversation about what is important, define what information might drive the group's decision making, and ensure that the group is clear about the purpose of its work. Equally valuable, a carefully devised action plan can provide the momentum for undertaking school and district change projects when participants return to work.

Action plans and updates can be part of follow-up training and a source of program evaluation data. As learning artifacts, action plans help track the impact of the training beyond attendance and participation and into what happens in schools and classrooms with students and teachers.

Encompassing more than the simple "things to do" list that many people use, action planning is actually a basic form of project management. In fact, a finished action plan "is so simple and straightforward that the power of the strategic thinking involved in developing it easily can be missed," notes consultant Robby Champion (2001, p. 62). Facilitating groups that are developing action plans requires stimulating members' thinking and helping them thoughtfully clarify each step.

Visioning Exercise

Any organization or individual must have a vision to be truly effective. A vision, in turn, is formed and supported by a set of shared beliefs. A clear vision goes beyond goals. A vision is much more grand and can guide goals and give them new meaning. Short- and long-term goals take an organization closer to the vision, or the dream that once seemed impossible. The dream becomes a reality.

Create a dream exercise. Explain that planning means having a vision. Have group members draw a picture of what the accomplished goal looks like. Gather group members in a circle. Give each one chart paper and a marker. Allow 5 to 10 minutes for all to draw what they would like to see themselves or the group to accomplish, or what the finished goal looks like. Invite each member to present the vision at the end of the exercise. After all have had a turn, discuss what the visions have in common, whether the dream is achievable, and how to accomplish it. Then begin to set SMART goals.

There are several steps to developing an action plan:

- Analyze the problem and the issues
- Define goals
- Identify objectives
- Identify obstacles
- Develop strategies
- List action steps and timelines
- Implement the action plan
- Assess the solution

ANALYZE THE PROBLEM

Many groups at the stage of developing action plans will already have been working together for some time before needing to create an action plan. Acting boards; standing committees, such as department teams; or ongoing work groups, such as districtwide curriculum committees, are examples of these kinds of ongoing groups.

First, these groups need to clearly define the issue the action plan will address, using the steps described in Chapter 1 for determining whether to have a meeting. They include defining the plan's purpose, writing a problem statement, as well as defining the nonpurpose, which will add clarity to the group's goal.

Tip: Clearly define how many meetings the group will spend on planning and how long each meeting will last to help define limits for the group.

Groups formed to address a specific issue will already have a clear goal. If they have followed the outline in this book, they may already have a written mission statement and perhaps defined and weighed their options and even determined the best course of action.

Define the Problem

For many, the toughest part of action planning is clearly defining problems to tackle systematically. Not everything standing in the way of student achievement is a solvable problem under the group's purview, so the facilitator's guidance and use of explicit examples are essential to help participants state the problem. One way to get clear about this issue is to write a goal statement that clearly outlines the current and the desired states.

Effective goals are SMART:

- Specific, data driven
- Measurable and observable
- Attainable, realistic, focused
- Results oriented, focused on student achievement
- Timebound

The goal usually answers the questions *who* will do *what* as *measured by* and by *when*. The facilitator can help the group begin its goal statement by pairing participants for 30 to 45 minutes of collegial help as they work to define the problem. The first step is to analyze available data focusing on the areas of strength and the areas of need. Examining student data is a critical first step. Looking at district, state, and local data, trends and report card data are important. It is important for each group to be conscious of two parts of the goal-writing process: where we are today ("as is") and where we want to be ("target"). Teams must make a commitment to a date so that the group has a concrete idea of what they will accomplish, and by when. The facilitator can encourage group members to act as critical friends during the data analysis process. Each person listens and jots down notes (or creates a web), while the other member of the pair talks through the problem. The speaker then switches, and the other person takes notes. After listening and questioning, the two should help each other clearly state the challenge, then check the problem statement against the five criteria for effective goals. Each pair's statement can be read and discussed by the group as a whole until the issue is defined.

Two other processes can also help the group define the issues, ask questions, identify concerns, and set goals to move forward to accomplish the group's purpose.

- *Common Response.* Give an index card to each participant. Ask each person to write his or her understanding of the purpose of the work. Collect the cards and read them aloud to ensure that everyone has an opportunity to contribute to the process. Encourage group members to discuss different perspectives and to acknowledge similarities and differences. From the cards and discussion, identify common threads. Write each common theme on chart paper for the group to see and use. Then review and build a statement that clarifies the intent and encompasses all of the contributions.

- *Pyramid.* This process works with larger groups, such as when the working group is responsible for writing the mission. Give each participant an index card on which he or she writes a statement of purpose. Next, have team members pair up. Ask each team of two to build one goal or mission statement using the best ideas from each

Tip: Review decision-making authority as outlined in Chapter 4 and discuss to what extent (advisory or decision making) the existing group has the authority to act on the issue facing the group.

person's first statement. One pair then joins with another pair to become a group of four. This group repeats the process, comparing the two statements and selecting the best of each to create one improved statement. Continue increasing the size of each group until the large group has two or three statements. Write the statements on chart paper and facilitate a large-group agreement of the statement. This process ensures that each person's voice influences the final product.

Goal statements should have a clear link to student achievement and should challenge current practice in a way that will lead to improvement. Good goal statements answer the following questions:

- Who is affected?
- What do you want them to achieve?
- How will you measure the progress?
- When will you achieve the target goal?
- What is the current level of performance?
- What is the goal for improvement?

Some groups find it helpful to state the issue in two parts: (1) what is the *current* state of the problem, or the starting point, and (2) what will be the *desired,* targeted state. For example, an "as is" statement might be as follows: 54% of fourth-grade students scored proficient or mastery on the fourth-grade writing competency test during the 2005/2006 school year. The *desired* outcome statement might be this: 70% of fourth-grade students will score proficient or above on the fourth-grade writing competency test during the 2007/2008 school year.

Or a goal statement might read like this: 100% of our students will achieve one-year growth on the state assessment, as measured by moving from proficient or above in seventh-grade math assessment to proficient or above in the eighth-grade math assessment, from June 2006 to June 2007.

Identify Obstacles

Identifying what forces keep any problem from being solved is an obvious step in addressing the problem. In *The Winning Trainer* (2001), Julius E. Eitington explains force field analysis as the process of approaching a problem or situation by first diagnosing its underlying forces. This is achieved by determining the driving forces (those forces favorable to the desired goal) and the restraining forces (those forces unfavorable to the desire goal).

A useful tool for identifying impediments is the *force field analysis* (Handout 5.1: Force Field Analysis provides a form for this). The

HANDOUT 5.1: FORCE FIELD ANALYSIS

Issue: _____

Current State: _____   **Desired State:** _____

_____   _____

(Make a list of things that are helping you achieve your goal.) → ← *(Make a list of things that are hindering the achievement of your goal.)*

_____   _____

_____   _____

_____   _____

_____   _____

_____   _____

_____   _____

_____   _____

_____   _____

_____   _____

_____   _____

_____   _____

_____   _____

_____   _____

> ## Identify Assumptions and Values
>
> Group members may want to spend some time discussing their assumptions and values. An assumption is a belief whose truth status is uncertain; it may or may not be true. When we make an assumption, we work as though that idea or perspective is the truth. Some groups make assumptions that may not be true, or groups may find that members hold competing assumptions. By identifying assumptions, the group is able to work more strategically, since members can recognize common values.
>
> Values are the principles or ideals that are important or desirable to an individual or group. They guide teamwork.
>
> Making agreements about the positive values or assumptions that will guide the work of the group is a powerful strategy.
>
> The following are some examples of assumptions:
>
> - Decisions will be student centered.
> - Every teacher will choose to teach every class after reviewing the composition of the class lists.
> - Every new teacher in this school will have the opportunity to be successful with the class they are assigned.
> - Every child deserves to have a highly effective teacher.
> - Every child deserves to be in a class with classmates who value learning.

facilitator draws a line down the center of a chart paper. The left side represents the current situation and is labeled "what is." The right side is the "desired" state.

The facilitator reminds group members of the rules of brainstorming and asks participants to identify helping forces: factors, issues, values, and programs that can help the group reach its desired state. A recorder writes these on the left side of the chart. The group then identifies constraints or hindering forces: factors, issues, values, and programs that keep the group from achieving the desired state, and these are recorded on the right.

The following are some examples of constraints:

- Forty percent of our students are English Language Learners, and they speak 14 different languages.
- Our school will have seven new teachers next year, including four first-year teachers.
- Class sizes are controlled by contractual language.
- The school will exceed its recommended capacity by 120 students.

Some groups assess the relative strengths of both helping and hindering forces using a numeric rating scale. You may use a scale (e.g., 5 = *very strong;* 4 = *strong;* 3 = *medium;* 2 = *low;* and 1 = *weak*) to evaluate the relative impact of the forces. Others use a graphic representation of proportionately sized arrows.

The group may analyze the forces using filters that the group determines. Forces could be economic, social, technological, political, educational, or environmental. The group may also find it helpful to discuss how the issues relate to the organization's mission and values.

The facilitator then helps the group refine their list of helping and hindering forces by examining them for their current effect. Some of them may no longer be effective as they once were, or they may have outlived their usefulness.

The group may then discuss how to decrease the number or strength of the forces that are hindering progress (eliminate the negative) and increase the impact of the forces that are supporting successful implementation (accentuate the positive). Many times a group finds that attending to the hindering forces and relieving some of the concerns will help the group make progress toward its goal.

Once the analysis is complete, your group can use this information to generate potential solutions. Explore the following:

- How to increase the number or strength of the helping forces.
- How to decrease the number or strength of the hindering forces.

The force field concept can be confusing, so it is taught in two steps: First, work to diagnose and understand a problem. Demonstrate an analysis on a real problem and diagram it. Have participants identify "restraining forces" that prevent solving the problem. Encourage the group to focus on major hurdles, such as lack of time, unavailability of materials, and power struggles among staff members. Second, identify the driving forces propelling the work on the problem—either positive or negative.

For example, a restraining force might be "I don't have time within my workday to address this issue." A driving force might be "My principal or superintendent wants this accomplished this year," or "Our school improvement effort requires that this problem be solved now."

Participants often complete the force field analysis and then set it aside because they don't know what to do with it. Force field analysis data become the ingredients for developing action steps. The group then uses a strategy, such as nominal group process, paired comparisons (described in Chapter 4), or another ranking process, to identify which helping or hindering forces merit the response of an action. For every training force the group feels has merit, the plan must include steps to address it.

I have used this tool successfully with many groups. Once, I supported a board of education that used the tool to identify all

> **Tip:** Save the notes from the force field analysis. These may prove valuable if the group needs to revisit the rationale for a decision. Groups may also continue working to resolve the restraining forces.

of the successes of the school district and all of its challenges. The board used dots as a simple prioritizing process and ultimately used the data from this group activity to write their goals.

Another group identified all of the reasons why parents were actively participating in parent/teacher activities and also identified all of the barriers to their participation. Once group members identified the barriers, they realized that many of the issues could easily be resolved, and they quickly identified action steps to resolve the identified barriers. In doing so, they resolved the challenges and opened the door to many more parents who eagerly wanted to participate.

Action Planning Steps

All good action planning follows the same process. Group members should proceed as follows:

1. Understand the problem and goals clearly in order to consider a variety of actions.

2. Create many possible solutions to the problem. A solution that hasn't been discussed can't be used.

3. Project the likely outcome of each option. Look for synergistic ways of combining several promising solutions into potent solutions.

4. Weigh the pros and cons of each course of solution and choose one to which the group can commit fully.

DEVELOP STRATEGIES

With the goal or purpose clearly posted for all group members to see, the facilitator or group leader should help group members agree on the root causes of the problem before the group begins to discuss solutions. Identifying underlying causes is an important part of addressing the issue. Without recognizing possible causes, group members will not be able to create solutions that will have an impact on the problem and lead to the desired outcome.

A helpful tool at this stage is the "fishbone" (See Handout 5.2: Fishbone Analysis). Cause-and-effect charts are called fishbones because they look like the bones of a fish when they are drawn on the chart. They are sometimes called "Ishikawa diagrams," after their inventor, Dr. Kaoru Ishikawa, a Japanese quality control statistician. The technique gives a group a systematic way of looking at possible causes. It can also be used for solutions or effects, but it is most often used to identify the possible causes. Once the possible causes are uncovered, a group can collect data to confirm or deny the hypothesis.

The problem is diagrammed from the perspective of the current condition, the problem that you want to correct, or the "goal," the conditions you want to exist when you have solved the problem. Cause-and-effect diagrams are most useful when the problem has

(Text continues on page 162)

HANDOUT 5.2: FISHBONE ANALYSIS

Comments to the Facilitator

A fishbone is a diagrammatic tool to help a group analyze the causes and effects of a certain problem. Cause-and-effect charts are called fishbones because of their shape. They are sometimes called Ishikawa diagrams after their inventor, Kaoru Ishikawa, a Japanese quality control statistician.

The cause-and-effect technique gives a group a systematic way of looking at causes or solutions. The problem can be diagrammed from the perspective of the "as is" state, the problem that you want to correct, or the "desired state," what conditions you want to exist when you have solved the problem.

Cause-and-effect diagrams are most useful when the process is clearly described and the problem has been clearly defined. When the problem is clearly stated, the factors contributing to the problem or the possible solutions will be much easier to generate.

Remember that fishbones only identify *possible* causes. When everyone agrees on the possible causes, data need to be collected to provide evidence of the actual causes.

When used for planning purposes, the cause-and-effect diagram focuses attention on a desired result. The main arrow points to what you want to happen, while the bones represent the steps/ideas needed to achieve the result.

This activity builds on a brainstorming process. In this activity, participants see how various causes relate to each other.

Preparation

Using chart paper, prepare large, blank fishbones for the total group (or sub-groups if that is appropriate) and mount them on the walls.

Directions

1. Write the problem statement—the effect of the process—in the rectangular box at the head of the "fish."

(Continued)

Handout 5.2 (Continued)

2. Identify the categories or major factors that contribute to the problem. Categories might include State/District, School, Teacher, Home, Student, and Demographics. Another fishbone might have "bone ends" including Demographics, Professional Development, Curriculum, Student Needs, and Staff Needs. Other more generic formats might have the major bones entitled People, Products, Price, and Promotion or Man, Machine, Materials, Methods, and Environment.

3. Have participants randomly identify possible causes in each of the categories using a brainstorming process. Gather the ideas and post them on the fish.

4. Silently, participants should group the sticky notes into categories. (Since they have heard these ideas expressed already, this process should take only a few minutes.)

5. Lead a discussion about the groupings until the group reaches a consensus on how to label each category.

6. After participants agree on the groupings, each group should be labeled. Write those labels into the rectangular boxes at the outer edges of the fish skeleton.

An example of a diagram is shown below.

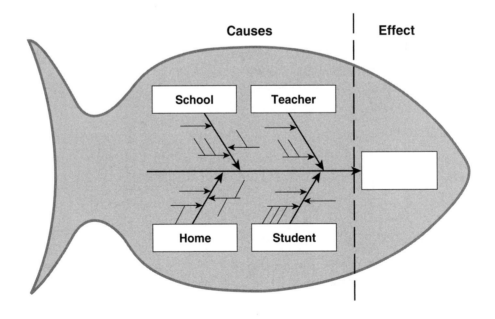

SOURCE: Adapted from *Leadership Through Quality: Interactive Skills Manual*, Rochester, NY: Xerox Corporation, 1986.

Fishbone Diagram

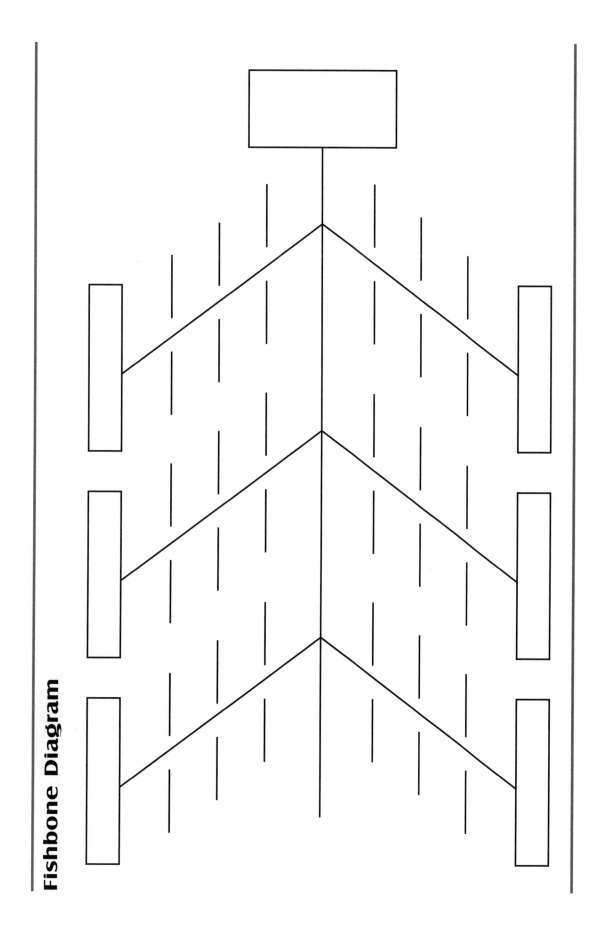

been clearly defined and the process is clearly described. When the problem is clearly stated, the factors contributing to the problem or the possible solutions are much easier to generate.

Remember that fishbones identify *possible* causes or solutions. On a chart to identify the possible causes, the central arrow points to the clearly stated problem, and the bones represent the possible causes for that problem. On a chart to identify solutions, the central arrow points to the desired outcome, and the "bones" represent the steps needed to achieve the result. The group leader or facilitator can aid the group in identifying the relative priority of causes using a simple vote for each "bone" of the diagram (use the form in Handout 5.3: Identifying Priorities).

Once key causes are identified, the facilitator leads the discussion about strategies that address the issue. A strategy states the purpose and action that will be implemented to meet the goal. Groups may address this step on a later agenda, and spend time between meetings collecting data to verify the identified causes or gathering additional information to confirm or extend their insights. This is important, since strategies and activities generally are written in direct response to issues that have been identified through data analysis, such as a content area the group identified as weak when analyzing student data.

> **Tip:** Groups typically write five to seven strategies for a goal.

> **Tip:** Be certain to have clear support, through direct involvement or a visible direction, from the appropriate high-level administrators to ensure that the planning process is supported and the results are valued.

Strategies also might be designed to address the needs of a No Child Left Behind group identified when the group disaggregated test data. For example, the team might identify a specific initiative to meet the needs of a group of students with learning disabilities.

Sample Strategies for a Goal

This is the goal:

- The percentage of students in sixth through eighth grades who score basic and above in English Language Arts (ELA), as measured by the ELA assessment, will increase from 63% in 2006 to 69% by May 2008.
- Strategies might include the following:
  - Writing across the curriculum (if data identified weak performance in writing)
  - Vocabulary development (if data identified weak performance in vocabulary)
  - Test-taking strategies (based on data)
  - Working with students with learning disabilities (if the disaggregated data report an achievement gap for students with disabilities)
  - Using technology to support the writing process (to enable students to write, edit, and revise)
  - Extending the day to give students special guided practice sessions
  - Family involvement (describe how parents, community members may support reading, writing, speaking, listening achievement)

HANDOUT 5.3: IDENTIFYING PRIORITIES

Comments to the Facilitator

This activity provides an efficient way to identify the priority causes. At the end of this activity, participants should be ready to begin developing action plans for their priority causes. (Remember that this is an informal process. Formal statistical analyses are needed to identify causal factors.)

Directions

MINOR CAUSE

1. Ask the group to vote on each cause on the bones of the fishbone diagram (see Handout 5.2). (If a large group has subdivided into smaller groups, each small group should select a new facilitator.)

2. Point to each cause and read it aloud. Instruct participants to vote in this way:

   - Minor cause: one finger
   - Average cause: three fingers
   - Major cause: five fingers

AVERAGE CAUSE

3. Count the number of fingers for each cause and record the count next to the item on the diagram. Priority causes are items that received the greatest number of votes.

4. Identify between 5 and 10 causes that received the most votes. Post the sticky notes with those causes down one side of the chart paper. (Note: Every group should decide in advance how many causes to include on its priority list. These will become the focus of the group's action plans.)

5. On a separate piece of paper, ask participants to silently prioritize causes by assigning a number 1-6 to each cause, with 6 being the most significant cause.

MAJOR CAUSE

6. Collect the rankings and calculate the average for each cause. Re-order the sticky notes according to the group's ranking.

SOURCE: Reprinted with permission from *Tools for Schools*, February/March 1998. Adapted from a presentation by James Cunningham, Educational Consultant, National School Services, Wheeling, Ill., During the 1997 NSDC Annual Conference.

The group narrows its priorities using a list reduction or other strategies for decision making, described in Chapter 4 (criteria rating, dots, balance sheet, weighted voting, paired comparisons, nominal group process).

Tip: Listing needed resources (such as funding, approval, or training) helps participants be realistic about the action plan. Create a budget to go along with the plan.

LIST ACTION STEPS AND TIMELINE

Now that the group has decided on strategies, members should define the *action* steps that need to be taken to implement the strategy. Action planning requires carefully laying out how goals will be accomplished, with specific results for each step. Therefore reaching a goal typically involves accomplishing a set of objectives along the way.

Tip: Action plans vary in the detail they include. Include as much detail as group members feel they need, based on their history of working together, current common understanding, the number of people involved in implementing the plan, the complexity of the strategy, and so on.

Each strategy is often associated with an activity, which is one of the methods needed to reach the desired outcome. Implementing a strategy involves a set of activities. In that sense, an activity is still a strategy, with the detail that will guide implementation.

Break Strategies Into Activities

- Activities list the steps that need to be taken by the group to fully implement the strategy. They are usually written with an action verb that states the steps to be taken.
- Activities might include professional development, scientifically based research, innovation initiatives, and so on.
- In an outline format, the strategy would be the key idea, the Roman numeral I; the activities would be the plan of action, detailed step-by-step as A, B, C, D, and E in the outline.

Tip: The timeline for the plan should begin as soon as possible but not later than a few weeks or the plan may be shelved and forgotten. Complete the plan in at most two to three months to maintain momentum.

Action planning includes specifying responsibilities and timelines with dates for each objective. This helps the group leader hold the group and members accountable for accomplishing the objective and monitoring their progress along the way.

The most effective plans should also include methods to monitor and evaluate outcomes, which includes knowing how the organization will know who has done what, and by when. (Use Handout 5.4: Action Planning Formats for worksheets to assist in this planning.)

It is also important to be able to identify progress or incremental measures. Be sure to include student outcomes whenever possible. Progress measures may include student behavior, teacher behavior, student performance/assessment data, changes in the environment, and/or qualitative data.

> **Tip:** Be sure each action step is clearly assigned to a responsible party and has a completion date listed on the timeline to avoid confusion and lack of implementation.

IMPLEMENT THE ACTION PLAN

When groups have spent as much time and consideration as a thoughtfully designed action plan requires, they will tend to want to begin a full-scale change effort immediately. For groups with very broad, systemic, long-term goals, it may be helpful to begin with a small group, such as with a department or school, before bringing the project to full scale. The team can then learn from the experience and modify before full implementation.

As the project is implemented, group members can collect information about successes and fine-tune the process. They will also be able to collect data about strategies that need modification so that subsequent steps will be more likely to succeed.

Communication is an essential element of implementation. Regular sharing of information at strategic points throughout the process with key stakeholders, from those supporting the project with resources to those with higher-level responsibility to school or district community stakeholders, not only keeps everyone updated, but serves to keep the group members motivated and looking for ways to support achieving the goals. Stakeholders not immediately involved in the action steps may need succinct summaries of the group's goals as a reminder of what the group is doing and why. These updates are an excellent opportunity to celebrate milestones.

There is no action plan that is set in stone. In fact, it is best to see it as a living, breathing document. These are some of the ways to keep it "alive" instead of becoming yet another "shelf plan":

- Revisit it often to monitor progress on each of the proposed strategies/actions.
- Identify blockages to any of the strategies or activities and determine what changes need to be made to ensure the achievement of the goals.
- When challenges arise, and they will, be sure to modify the plan, adjust timelines, or assign the activity to a new champion.
- Collect local data to give you regular information regarding progress toward the achievement of your goals.

HANDOUT 5.4: ACTION PLANNING FORMATS

Action Planning Format 1

Project: _____

Task	Talent *(Person Responsible)*	Timeline

Action Planning Format 2

Create headings that will help your group in the planning and monitoring process.

Goal: _____

Task	Talent *(Person Responsible)*	Budget	Timeline	Progress Indicators/ Status

(Continued)

Handout 5.4 (Continued)

ACTION PLANNING FORMAT 3

Goal: _____

Strategy/Activity	Lead and Staff Person	Target Dates (Beginning and Ending)	Resources	Professional Development Activities/Needs	Indicators of Progress Midyear

- Determine priorities for budgeting and discuss how to find and allocate resources for high priorities.
- Take opportunities to celebrate milestones and accomplishments.

ASSESS THE SOLUTION

The planning process is never complete—once a strategy is implemented, the group must constantly assess progress. On a regular basis, the leader or facilitator should ask the group, "How is it going?"

Tracking progress can be done in myriad ways: keeping a log, assembling an album of pictures or student work samples, or collecting agendas or notes from team meetings.

Another important means of monitoring progress is to agree to a set of quantifiable measures that define successful implementation of specific actions. These "milestones" can be written into the action plan and marked along the timeline. Envisioning milestones and ways to check progress keeps the work on the action plan focused.

Participants often wonder about the difference between a milestone and an action step. Clarifying the difference between the two is important so that the group members have a common understanding of the language they use when they are working together. For example, a milestone might be completing an important set of guidelines, distributing a survey, gaining consensus on a big issue, or holding an important event. An action plan might have 6 to 12 strategic milestones, with dates aligned to key events. The group should have clearly specified an individual to be responsible for the milestone. That person may not be responsible for all the work, but may have responsibility for communicating progress toward the milestone and specifically recognizing when it is achieved. I like to say that each strategy or activity has a champion, the "go to" person.

Tip: Long-term action plans often are revised during their course, and dates can be adjusted. Milestones should not be clubs hanging over participants' heads, but causes for celebration when achieved.

Assessing the action plan at periodic intervals helps the group accomplish the goal and ensures that it gets done in a timely fashion. At the end of the project period, the leader or facilitator should ask the group to assess the following:

- Was the problem solved?
- How well did the solution work?
- Was the solution effective?
- Did we reach the goal (desired state, target)?
- Did we create other problems?

Using the information gathered during the evaluation stage, the group begins the process again, creating an ongoing cycle that allows the group to be committed to continuous improvement.

Planning is an essential process in improving a school or organization. Whether it is a simple list of things to do, a "task/talent/timeline" plan, or a complex strategic plan aligning and focusing the work of a large organization, planning is the way we identify our goals and how we plan to achieve them. In the context of groups solving problems together, action planning is a key part of the cycle of groups forming for common purposes, finding ways to collaborate effectively, making meaningful decisions, and ultimately implementing and assessing effective solutions.

Conclusion

When I first began to teach people about meeting processes, I began each seminar by saying, "Repeat after me . . . *We have too many meetings.*" The group would laugh and loudly repeat the sentence once, twice, or sometimes three times.

It seems that everyone shares the experience of participating in far too many unproductive meetings. It is a common refrain whenever I talk to people about the greatest frustration in their work.

I learned the tools in this book out of self-preservation. I did not want to spend my career in endless meetings with poorly defined goals. Each time I confronted another team or meeting challenge, I accepted it as an opportunity to consider alternative ways to respond. And over the course of 20 years, I have built this tool kit, filled with processes to help build relationships, achieve meeting objectives, save time, and reduce the frustration that so many terrific educators face each and every day.

I believe that collaborative work ensures success. When faced with simple or complex tasks that require teamwork, I slow down and ask myself and the team some of the questions that I have outlined in this book.

I hope that these ideas resonate for you and that you will experiment and find the ones that help you have meaningful interactions with one another, save time, solve problems, make good decisions, resolve conflicts, make agreements, and help your teams serve the children of your community.

Those of you who know me personally will recall that I always use my closing as an opportunity to remind participants in my seminars to take care of themselves. I will do the same here: I hope you save enough time by holding more productive meetings so that you can spend it with the people you love—your parents, your partners, your children, and your friends. Take care of yourself. Remember, the children of your community need you to be your very best.

References

Arbuckle, M. A., & Murray, L. D. (1989). *Building systems for professional growth: An action guide.* Providence, RI: Regional Lab for Educational Improvement of the Northeast and Islands and the Maine Department of Education & Cultural Services.

Bertagnoli, L. (1999, September 13). Meeting expectations of high productivity. *Crain's Chicago Business.*

Blake, R., & Mouton, J. (1985). *The managerial grid: The key to successful leadership.* Houston, TX: Gulf Publishing.

Blosser, P. E. (1997). *How to ask the right questions.* Arlington, VA: National Science Teachers Association.

Champion, R. (2001, Fall). Planning for action, step by step. *Journal of Staff Development, 22*(4), 62–63.

Dolan, W. P. (1994). *Restructuring our schools: A primer on systemic change.* Kansas City, MO: Systems & Organization.

Eaker, R., DuFour R., & DuFour, R. (2002). *Getting started: Reculturing school to become professional learning communities.* Bloomington, IN: National Educational Service.

Eitington, J. (2001). *The winning trainer: Winning ways to involve people in learning.* Burlington, MA: Butterworth-Heinemann.

Fullan, M. (2001). *Leading in a culture of change.* San Francisco: Jossey-Bass.

Garmston, R. J. (2000, Winter). Developer's toolbox isn't complete without a good question. *Journal of Staff Development, 21*(1), 73–75.

Garmston, R. J. (2002a, Fall). *Collective ownership is the key to effectiveness. Journal of Staff Development, 23*(4), 76–77.

Garmston, R. J. (2002b, Winter). The 5 principles of successful meetings. *Journal of Staff Development, 23*(1), 66–67.

Garmston, R. J. (2005a, Spring). Group wise: Create a culture of inquiry and develop productive groups. *Journal of Staff Development, 26*(2), 65–66.

Garmston, R. J. (2005b, Fall). Group Wise: No time for learning? Just take it in tiny bites and savor it. *Journal of Staff Development, 26*(4), 65.

Garmston, R. J., & Wellman, B. (1999). *The adaptive school: A sourcebook for developing collaborative groups.* Norwood, MA: Christopher-Gordon.

Hirsh, S., Delehant, A., & Sparks, S. (1994). *Keys to successful meetings.* Oxford, OH: National Staff Development Council.

Hoffman, C., & Ness, J. (1998). *Putting sense into consensus.* Tacoma, WA: VISTA Associates.

Janis, I. L. (1971, November). Groupthink. *Psychology Today, 5*(6), 43–44, 46, 74–76.

Jensen, E. (1998). *Teaching with the brain in mind.* Alexandria, VA: ASCD.

Katzenbach, J., & Smith, D. (1986). *The wisdom of teams.* Boston: Harvard Business Review Press.

Kayser, T. (1990). *Mining group gold.* El Segundo, CA: Serif.

Kayser, T. (1994). *Building team power: How to unleash the collaborative genius of work teams.* Burr Ridge, IL: Irwin Professional.

MCI Conferencing. (1998). *Meetings in America: A study of trends, costs and attitudes toward business travel, teleconferencing, and their impact on productivity.* MCI

Conferencing white paper, prepared by INFOCOM. Retrieved May 26, 2006, from http://e-meetings.mci.com/meetingsinamerica/uswhitepaper.php.

Michalko, M. (1991). *Thinkertoys.* Berkeley, CA: Ten Speed Press.

Microsoft Corporation. (2005, March). *Survey finds workers average only three productive days per week.* Retrieved May 26, 2006, from www.microsoft.com/presspass/press/2005/mar05/03–15ThreeProductiveDaysPR.mspx.

Murphy C., & Murphy, M. (2004). Study groups. In L. B. Easton (Ed.), *Powerful designs for professional learning.* Oxford, OH: National Staff Development Council.

Paul, R., & Elder. L. (2004). *The miniature guide to critical thinking: Concepts and tools.* Dillon Beach, CA: Foundation for Critical Thinking.

Richardson, J. (1999, August/September). Norms put the "Golden Rule" into practice for groups. *Tools for Schools.*

Richardson, J. (2004, April/May). Consensus: Arrive at agreement—agreeably. *Tools for Schools,* pp. 1–2.

Rogers, E. M., & Rogers, E. (2003). *Diffusion innovations* (5th ed.). New York: Free Press.

Scannell, E. E., & Newstrom, J. W. (1980). *Games trainers play.* Columbus, OH: McGraw-Hill.

Scannell, E. E., & Newstrom, J. W. (1994). *Even more games trainers play.* Columbus, OH: McGraw-Hill.

Schwarz, R. (1994). *The skilled facilitator: Practical wisdom for developing effective groups.* San Francisco: Jossey-Bass.

Sparks, D. (2005). *Leading for results: Transforming teaching, learning, and relationships in schools.* Thousand Oaks, CA: Corwin Press.

Xerox Corporation. (1986). *Leadership through quality: Interactive skills manual.* Rochester, NY: Author.

Extended Readings

Bliss, E. (1986). *Getting things done.* New York: Bantam Books.

Block, P. (1991). *Flawless consulting.* San Diego, CA: University Associates.

Bradford, L. (1976). *Making meetings work: A guide for leaders and group members.* San Diego, CA: Pfeiffer.

Brandt, R. (1987). On cooperation in schools: A conversation with David and Roger Johnson. *Educational Leadership, 45*(3), 14–19.

Champion, R. (1993). *Tools for change workshops.* Oxford, OH: National Staff Development Council.

Champion, R. (2000). *Learning the craft of training.* Oxford, OH: National Staff Development Council.

Covey, S. (1989). *Seven habits of highly effective people.* New York: Simon & Schuster.

Covey, S. (1990). *Principle-centered leadership.* New York: Simon & Schuster.

DeBono, E. (1992). *Serious creativity.* New York: Harper Business.

Doyle, M., & Straus, D. (1993). *How to make meetings work.* New York: Berkley Publishing Group.

Eller, J. (2004). *Effective group facilitation in education: How to energize meetings and manage difficult groups.* Thousand Oaks, CA: Corwin Press.

Eller, S. (2005). *Energizing staff meetings.* Thousand Oaks, CA: Corwin Press.

Fisher, R., & Ury, W. (1983). *Getting to yes.* New York: Bantam Books.

Forbes-Greene, S. (1983). *The encyclopedia of icebreakers: Structured activities that warm up, motivate, challenge, acquaint, and energize.* San Diego, CA: Pfeiffer.

Garmston, R. J. (1997). *The presenter's fieldbook: A practical guide.* Norwood, MA: Christopher-Gordon.

Garmston, R. J. & Wellman, B. (1999). *The adaptive school: A sourcebook for developing collaborative groups.* Norwood, MA: Christopher-Gordon.

Goodman, P. S. (1986). *Designing effective workgroups.* San Francisco: Jossey-Bass.

Hess, K. (Ed.). (1987). *Creating the high performance team.* New York: Wiley.

Hirsh, S. (1997, April). Keeping your school improvement plan on track. *School Team Innovator.*

Hirsh, S., & Murphy, M. (1991). *School improvement planning manual.* Oxford, OH: National Staff Development Council.

Johnson, D. W., & Johnson, R. T. (1987). *Joining together: Group theory and group skills* (3rd ed.). Englewood Cliffs, NJ: Prentice Hall.

Kegan, R., & Laskow Lahey, L. (2002). *How the way we talk can change the way we work: Seven languages for transformation.* San Francisco: Jossey-Bass.

Killion, J. E., & Delehant, A. (1992). *Facilitator's fun kit.* Oxford, OH: National Staff Development Council.

Lacoursier, R. (1980). *The life cycle of groups* (2nd ed.). New York: Human Sciences Press.

Little, J. W. (1982). Norms of collegiality and experimentation: Workplace conditions of school success. *American Educational Research Journal, 19,* 325–340.

Miles, M. B. (1981). *Learning to work in groups* (2nd ed.). New York: Teachers College Press.

Mundry, S. (2000). *Designing successful professional meetings and conferences in education.* Thousand Oaks, CA: Corwin Press.

Nelson, B., & Spitzer, D. R. (2002). *The 1001 rewards and recognition fieldbook: The complete guide.* New York: Workman.

Nilson, C. *Team games for trainers.* Columbus, OH: McGraw-Hill.

Olsen, W. R., & Sommers, W. A. (2005). *Energizing staff development using film clips: Memorable movie moments that promote reflection, conversation, and action.* Thousand Oaks, CA: Corwin Press.

Peters, T. (1987). *Thriving on chaos: Handbook for a management revolution.* New York: Knopf.

Sagor, R. (2004). *The action research guidebook: A four-step process for educators and school teams.* Thousand Oaks, CA: Corwin Press.

Scearce, C. (1992). *100 ways to build teams.* Thousand Oaks, CA: Corwin Press.

Schindler-Rainman, E., & Lippitt, R. (1988). *Taking your meetings out of the doldrums.* San Diego, CA: University Associates.

Scott, S. (2002). *Fierce conversations.* New York: The Berkeley Publishing Group.

Slavin, R. E. (1987). Cooperative learning and the cooperative schools. *Educational Leadership, 45*(3), 7–13.

Stiles, K. E., Mundry, S., & Kaser, J. (2005). *Facilitator's guide to leading every day* (2nd ed.). Thousand Oaks, CA: Corwin Press.

Stokes, S. (1981). *School-based staffed support teams.* Bloomington, IN: National Inservice Network, Indiana University.

Stone, D., Patton, B., Heen, S., & Fisher, R. (2000). *Difficult conversations: How to discuss what matters most.* New York: Penguin.

Ury, W. (1993). *Getting past no.* New York: Bantam Books.

Von Oech, R. (1990). *A whack on the side of the head.* New York: Warner Books.

Waterman, R. H. (1988). *The renewal factor.* New York: Bantam Books.

Weisbord, M. R. (1987). *Productive workplaces: Organizing and managing for dignity, meaning and community.* San Francisco: Jossey-Bass.

Wheelan, S. A. (2005). *Faculty groups: From frustration to collaboration.* Thousand Oaks, CA: Corwin Press.

Williams, R. B. (1993). *More than 50 ways to build team consensus.* Thousand Oaks, CA: Corwin Press.

Yankelovich, D. (1999). *The magic of dialogue: Transforming conflict into cooperation.* New York: Simon & Schuster.

Index

CORWIN PRESS

The Corwin Press logo—a raven striding across an open book—represents the union of courage and learning. Corwin Press is committed to improving education for all learners by publishing books and other professional development resources for those serving the field of PreK–12 education. By providing practical, hands-on materials, Corwin Press continues to carry out the promise of its motto: **"Helping Educators Do Their Work Better."**

NSDC's mission is to ensure success for all students by serving as the international network for those who improve schools and by advancing individual and organization development.